Arizmendi *Reflections*

Arizmendi with bicycle in Arrasate (or Mondragón), about 1955.

Among family, undated, as a young priest.

The cover draws on two often-reproduced photos (opposite), taken at different points in Arizmendi's life.

In North America, where this translation is published, a pair of pine trees is a symbol adopted among cooperatives for many years to represent themselves and their ideals. Like people, it's observed, pines thrive best when they grow not singly but together. The tree stands in this way for the wisdom of building in community.

It's this wisdom, not one man's alone but a wisdom experienced commonly in a real community's history of shared life, that it is hoped the reader will find evidence of in these pages—and be encouraged, then, to keep seeking beyond them.

# Reflections

## José María Arizmendiarrieta

*Selected and Compiled by*
*Joxe Azurmendi*

*Translated by*
*The Interpreters' Cooperative*
*of Madison*

SOLIDARITY HALL

Rights to the original text compiled by Joxe Azurmendi are held by Otalora, the cooperative development organization of Mondragon Cooperative Corporation in Guipúzcoa, Spain. This translation is published by permission.

Publication team:

| | |
|---:|---|
| translation | Steve Herrick |
| | Eric Rohland |
| | Julio García |
| | Matt Noyes |
| | Naiara Bitorika |
| publishing/editorial | Elias Crim |
| design/production | Paul Bowman |
| | Esther West |
| | the members of Cooperatus |

Reflections of José María Arizmendiarrieta ©2022 by The Interpreters' Cooperative of Madison is licensed under the Creative Commons Attribution–ShareAlike 4.0 International License.

The book in its entirety may be copied, adapted, and distributed in any medium or format, where

- appropriate credit is given to this work's creators or contributors,
- a link to the original license is provided,
- any changes made are acknowledged,
- any adaptation of the work is distributed under the same license, and
- no restrictions are made beyond those specified under this license.

To view a copy of this license in full and for further information, visit:

http://creativecommons.org/licenses/by-sa/4.0/

Further rights to images and writing collected in this book may be retained separately by the respective contributors or creators. The license summarized above is provided in reference to the book as a whole.

# Contents

| | | |
|---|---|---|
| Translators' Preface  *Steve Herrick* | | vii |
| Foreword  *Nathan Schneider* | | xi |
| "Voices of Mondragón"  *David Herrera* | | xv |
| | | |
| Joxe Azurmendi Preface | | 3 |
| Opening | | 5 |

## 1. People and Society

### 1.1 THE PERSON
- 1.1.1 Personal Dignity — 11
- 1.1.2 The Person: Foundation and Purpose — 13
- 1.1.3 Ideals — 16
- 1.1.4 Man, Woman, Senior Citizen, Child — 18

### 1.2 FREEDOM
- 1.2.1 Freedom and Humanity — 23
- 1.2.2 Freedom and Solidarity — 24
- 1.2.3 Freedom and Discipline — 25
- 1.2.4 Cooperative Democracy — 27

### 1.3 RESPONSIBILITY
- 1.3.1 Responsibility and Self-Management — 29
- 1.3.2 Responsibility and Solidarity — 31

### 1.4 MORALS
- 1.4.1 Human Maturity — 35
- 1.4.2 Christianity — 39

### 1.5 EDUCATION
- 1.5.1 Culture and Personality — 43
- 1.5.2 Culture and Emancipation — 45
- 1.5.3 Education and Cooperativism — 50

## CONTENTS

### 1.6 THE SIGN OF VITALITY
- 1.6.1 "There Is Always One More Step to Take" — 53
- 1.6.2 Cooperativism Is an Experience — 55

## 2. Work and the Cooperative Enterprise

### 2.1 WORK
- 2.1.1 The Dignity of Work — 63
- 2.1.2 Humanizing Work — 66

### 2.2 UNITY
- 2.2.1 Human Foundation — 69
- 2.2.2 Economic Foundation — 71
- 2.2.3 Solidarity — 73

### 2.3 UTOPIA AND REVOLUTION
- 2.3.1 The Danger of Utopia — 79
- 2.3.2 Revolution — 81

### 2.4 REALISM AND A NEW ORDER
- 2.4.1 Rationality — 87
- 2.4.2 Vision of the Future — 90
- 2.4.3 The New Cooperative Order — 93

### 2.5 THE COOPERATIVE ENTERPRISE
- 2.5.1 The Cooperative Spirit — 97
- 2.5.2 Cooperative Management — 101
- 2.5.3 Workers and Entrepreneurs — 105
- 2.5.4 An Experience in Perpetual Development — 111

Afterword  *Jessica Gordon Nembhard* — 117

Bibliographical Note — 120

# Translators' Preface

*Steve Herrick*

To begin, we have to thank Professor Joxe Azurmendi for compiling this collection. He did so in 1980, four years after the death of Father Arizmendiarrieta (or "Arizmendi," not to be confused with Azurmendi). For his doctoral thesis, he took a fifteen-volume collection of Arizmendi's homilies, editorials, letters, articles, fliers, notebooks, journals, speeches, conference keynotes, meeting minutes, hand-written notes in the margins of books he was reading, and even train schedules and grocery lists, and boiled them down to a book that was still over 600 pages long. It was called *The Cooperative Man: Arizmendiarrieta's Thought*, and it is not available in English as of this writing. He then further distilled that down to a collection of quotes from Father Arizmendi, called *Pensamientos*, or, in English, *Reflections*. These were the first of numerous books he has written in Spanish and Basque.

We also thank the team led by David Herrera that originally translated *Pensamientos* into English. Years after it was published, we continue to see examples from it quoted regularly. It was the starting point for this new translation.

Next, we want to express our gratitude to Solidarity Hall for inviting us to work on this book. This is a historic document, and one that is close to our hearts, as members of a worker cooperative ourselves.

Our translation has endeavored to maintain the flavor of the writing of a priest who was highly educated but well grounded, who had served as a soldier but loved peace, and who called cooperation revolutionary in a sense that few understood at the time. He didn't invent the idea of the cooperative any more than the Rochdale Pioneers did, but he stands alongside them as a shining example of how powerful it can be. He arrived in Mondragon at age 26, with his few possessions in a cardboard box. He never did accumulate many worldly possessions (other than books), but rather, stored up his treasure in heaven. When he died, 35 years later, the congregants at his funeral filled the church, the plaza in front, and all the streets in every direction for many blocks. He had turned a remote, backwards, war-torn village deep in the hills of the Basque Country into a center of industry, and from there, it has grown into the global standard-bearer for worker cooperativism. This book contains a sampling of the words he used to accomplish this.

Speaking of the words, we have taken one editorial liberty in our translation. Like the large majority of writers in the middle of the 20th century, Arizmendi was embarrassingly and distractingly sexist by 21st-century standards. We have chosen to use gender-neutral terms throughout the text, except where gender itself is the topic of discussion. While some may see this as an overreach on our part, we feel it is consistent with the slow but steady evolution of Arizmendi's views on the role of women in society, some of which can be seen in these pages (for example, reflections 287, 288, and the second half of section 1.1.4). Given that he was on the forefront of so many economic and social issues in his day, we believe that today, he would want us to use language that was inclusive not only of women, but of LGBT+ people as well.

It has been an honor to do this translation, and we hope it will serve the movement for many years to come.

In cooperation,
The translation team:

*Steve Herrick*
*Eric Rohland*
*Julio García*
*Matt Noyes*
*Naiara Bitorika* (Basque)

With additional proofreading and advice from Nathan Schneider and Elias Crim.

# Foreword

*Nathan Schneider*

Countless aspiring imitators have visited and studied the Basque Country's Mondragon cooperatives, born not long after the war-torn 1940s, under the nose of fascist Spain. How many times have I heard that "model" brought up, in meetings of economic activists, from Melbourne to Oakland to webinar upon webinar, as the thing participants are trying to replicate? And yet still Mondragon stands: the world's largest worker-cooperative conglomerate, with upward of a hundred thousand employee owners—no imitators even close.

This little book provides an indication about why. Yes, the mighty Mondragon enterprises of manufacturing, retail, and finance carry out a model, an entrepreneurial scheme. The pay ratios, the mutual investment, the job protections, the mechanisms of self-governance—there is much for modelers to examine and export. Mondragon even has its own university and apostles abroad. And yet.

Father José María Arizmendiarrieta, the cooperatives' founder, was a priest through and through. His *Reflections* contain economic insights. But these aphorisms and fragments reveal that his central motivation was spiritual—not to the exclusion of the practical, but with the recognition that plutocratic capitalism, also, is a spiritual movement. Those who want to supplant the models of capitalism must also uproot its invasive spirit.

Arizmendi lived in one of those periods when the Catholic Church—if you knew where to look, and even despite itself—bore the means of social transformation. In 1891, Pope Leo XIII had published his encyclical Rerum Novarum, rebuking both rapacious capitalists and utopian communists, calling instead for a society that enables "as many as possible of the people to become owners." Catholics didn't invent modern cooperative business, but Pope Leo's vision for a society of universal, distributed ownership supercharged it. The cooperative idea of businesses owned and governed by those who use them—not outside investors just looking for a profit—seemed to many precisely the third way Pope Leo was looking for. It was neither crony capitalism nor state communism; it blended personal responsibility and solidarity. Since cooperatives tend to associate together rather than merge into monopolies, they practice the Catholic value of subsidiarity—keeping things under local control wherever possible.

Cooperative undertakings spread among Catholics, from cheese producers and artisans in northern Italy to the Desjardins system of Quebec, which traveled southward to seed the credit union movement in the United States. An architect of the New Deal, the economist-priest Monsignor John A. Ryan, called cooperatives "the mechanism and the atmosphere for a greater development of the altruistic spirit than is possible under any other economic system." Following the civil-rights movement, a leading architect of Black-owned cooperatives in the American South was Fr. Albert McKnight, a visionary pan-Africanist priest. Over and over, the pope's spiritual call produced uniquely successful entrepreneurship.

This legacy reached Pope Francis's accountant father, in Argentina, who told his son to appreciate cooperativism this way: "It goes forward slowly, but it is sure." The slowness is real; for a whole decade before his students opened their first business in 1956, Arizmendi patiently taught cooperative principles at his local technical school.

A concurrent strain of Catholic thought in the early 20th century was personalism—a kind of reverse existentialism that celebrates the intrinsic dignity of the human person, a being made in the image of God. The economic democracy of a cooperative invites that dignity to emerge, to bring out the divine imprint in each participant—as Arizmendi puts it, "granting ourselves permission to be considered free beings." That process of becoming ever more fully human is called formation. You'll encounter it in the pages that follow.

Do not, however, mistake Arizmendi's Catholicism for narrow sectarianism. He didn't. He inherits the Basque people's long practice of democracy and their struggles for independence. He was a journalist during the Spanish Civil War, when entire regions of the country operated under a well-organized anarchism of workers' assemblies, which were highly anti-clerical. Yet he fuses these influences into universal terms. His cooperative spirituality depends on no particular religious or national identity, while it draws from many.

Here is a book that belongs in the back pocket of aspiring cooperators, at least for a time in their formation, long enough to inoculate them from the allure of models. This great practitioner leaves no room for doubt that economic democracy is as much a matter of culture and spirit as any economics. And if Arizmendi is a saint, as some contend, perhaps this freshly translated collection of his wisdom will be a channel for new cooperative miracles.

## Voices of Mondragón

*David Herrera*

*In 2000, American academic David Herrera was visiting Mondragon to conduct doctoral thesis research on the cooperative's organization and workplace culture. In interviews with worker-owners, he was struck by their openness and the consistency of values expressed in their responses, especially in terms found in Catholic social thought: solidarity, social and economic justice, the dignity of the person and of human work.*

*"When ready to present my findings," Herrera wrote later, "I woke up one morning and ... what I had learnt during my interviews become a poem in my mind, which I called 'Voices of Mondragon.'"*

> "What is the essence of Mondragon?"
> "What is the Mondragon experience?"
> "What is its soul?"
> You ask.
> This I am not able to say,
> Not at this time ...
> But I know I can tell you
> What it all means to me.
>
> I'll never be rich,
> I'll never be poor.

I'll have all I need
And most that I want
And I'll have enough.
At least I will know
The work that I do
Will not just result
In having a few
Who already are rich
Get even richer!

We started small
Five men and a priest
(Don Josémaría
He was called),
Plus some others whose names are now lost.
Times were hard,
Resources few,
But trust, people had,
In these men
And their cause:
Jobs, education, better living for all.
My dad and his friends
Borrowed money
Mortgaged their homes,
And worked extra hours
To help with this venture:
A dream of a few, a hope of so many.
The idea was old
The meaning was new:
Treat your neighbor as yourself,
This now meant:
Participation,
Democracy,
Equality,
Solidarity —

In a system of justice that gives all a share.

I can have a say
About most things.
And this, I like
Though sometimes
I don't say anything …
Yet I know that
Where I work,
Nothing important happens without my vote.

One member/one vote
Is a rule, we say,
That gives us equality.
I know this is true
But, in my view,
What also makes us equal is that
My boss and I
Can talk about anything,
We may disagree,
We may even fight.
And then we part ways,
Meet on the street,
At the square,
Or at church,
Have a drink,
Have a talk.
Friends we still are, nothing has changed.

I am proud to be an owner
Of something special.
It is not what we do
It is that we care
For those that we know
And those that we don't.

—It is not charisma
That makes our leaders.
It is credibility,
Or rather, it's trust.

And some people say,
"Yes, I understand it all,
But who has the power?"
And then I reflect:
We are the owners.
We make the decisions.
We elect our leaders.
So I ask,
Who has the power?
For you know,
Really,
I am a leader…
And so is she…
And so is he…
And so are they.
Sometimes I lead,
Sometimes I follow.
But mostly
We all lead, we all follow, we do both together.
—I like to participate,
To vote,
To know that we are equal
In life and at work.
But I also know
I must be the one
Who makes these decisions:
To be educated,
To keep well informed,
Develop myself,
And keep up with all.

If I don't do this
I'll find that my vote,
My participation,
Won't help us at all.

We now have a big name:
Mondragon Corporación Cooperativa,
Or MCC.
"Sounds better," some say,
"than the quaint
'Mondragon experience.'"
For one thing I know:
What makes us, is not our name —
It's the way we look at a challenge:
We
Discuss it,
Discuss it,
Agree,
Disagree,
Discuss it,
Discuss it,
And then
We decide.
We change,
We change,
We evolve
We evolve together.
This is what keeps us alive — this is "the experience."

And I know this for sure
We need to make money
But,
We need to care too
For those who have less ...

I know that for sure.
Globalization is a need
I hear
We must now grow
In faraway places —
Too far to go.
You know,
I am beginning to think this is needed,
And so
I should let those who know
Decide what is best for us all.
Or should I?
I'd still like to know
How decisions are made
Since
When we lost money in Argentina
It's us that will pay.

"Solidarity," you say?
That word I don't use...
But let me tell you
What I think it means.
It means sacrifice
Of those at the top
So others like me
Can earn a bit more.
It means that we all
Share earnings with all
In good and bad times
We divide it all up.
It means that we share
Year in and year out
Part of our earnings
To help those without.
Sometimes it seems

I am like a Siamese twin:
The pain of another
I feel just as much.
And at times I feel
It is like we're all
Climbing a mountain
With only one rope.
We know very well
If one of us fails
Down we all go.

I think this is true
We care for each other
But I fear for the future
Because of the ghosts
That come with new words
Like "globalization."

But in spite of my fears
My doubts, my complains,
I prefer working here
And facing all those ghosts.
For we have a tradition
Of solving these things
By working together and finding a way.
Will this time be different?
I don't think so.
We will work through it all
As we always do.
Hard work, change,
Whatever it takes, I know we'll come through.

So you ask me
What is the soul of Mondragon?
I still don't know …

And thus cannot help you
To find our soul.
I can only tell you
What I feel we are
And what I feel we are not.
Utopia, we are not,
It's no paradise,
And we are no angels.
We are just people
Working and changing together
"building the road as we travel."

# REFLECTIONS

Great people take on their true dimensions when we can see them with enough perspective to take in their true human stature. With the passage of time, visionaries become noble, and the futilities of fashion invariably fade.

The passing of the years is a good measuring stick for evaluating the depth and success of good ideas.

The reprint of this booklet, which compiles some of the thoughts of Fr. José María Arizmendiarrieta, is an act of recognition and acceptance of his indisputable leadership.

> —*Joxe Azurmendi, short preface to the Spanish and Basque original edition*

Juventud Deportiva Mondragón assembly in the Cine Frontón-Gurea, undated.

The ideal of the Mondragon Youth is to make this town the model for the industrial towns of Guipúzcoa (1941).

Fr. Arizmendiarrieta in procession, undated.

This priest considers the domain of human realities to be within his purview when what he practices and preaches is simply the need for, and the nature of, a new spirit of justice and love.

This spirit can manifest itself in tangible realities on a human scale, in response to something beyond profit, greed, and narrow self-interest. In any case, we already know which side the blind and powerful forces are usually on. The people, the masses, the past, present, and future majority, may well find that they have more than a little justice, reason, and moral strength on their side, and yet, (…) their way is blocked "not by the lack of power, but the lack of knowledge."

This is what makes messengers of truth both perennial and timely, even if some may say that does not put food on the table. Messengers are needed, messages need to be objective, and the debate should not be so much who the messenger is as what the message says, since the message must be repeated to each generation.

# 1 People and Society

Prison camp, Spain, 1937. Arizmendiarrieta third from right.

# 1.1
# The Person

## 1.1.1 Personal Dignity

Justice cannot be practiced where human dignity is ignored.

People not only have stomachs and material needs, but also an increasingly well-defined awareness of their dignity.

People die not only from hunger and physical exhaustion, but also from boredom and sadness, and a lack of hope and joy in life.

A well-laden pantry does not satisfy the yearnings of a company employee.

Multiple reforms and, even more so, a change in mindset, are indispensable if economic activity is to achieve its human purpose. Humanity is ultimately the creator, the center, and the end of all economic and social life.

A social good must justify itself economically no less than an economic good must authenticate itself socially.

9   The question is whether we can live with dignity, and living with dignity is being able to provide for ourselves. With this in mind, no paternalism can ever satisfy us, nor can we, as free human beings, settle for any walled paradise.

10  The idea is to institutionalize integrity. Better yet, the idea is to institutionalize human greatness.

11  We live in the heart of a community, a town inhabited by people, not proletarians.

12  It is true that those who have the soul of a peon are better off as peons, but we must not think that it is only in the lower classes that the souls of peons are to be found.

13  Believing in dignity is not about protesting, but about respecting laws.

14  Goodness and justice, wherever they may be found, whatever color they are wrapped in, cry out to be embraced and accepted. The person who does not do this is not human, much less Christian.

15  Freedom, independence, and personality constitute, in the innermost part of human beings that we call conscience, that which is most inherently human, the most intimate self.

16  A prosperous and stable society is one that is made up of living institutions that are guided by the conscience of free and intelligent people. To develop citizens, we would do well to start by considering everyone with whom we want to collaborate in the endeavor to be such people.

## 1.1.2 The Person: Foundation and Purpose

All economic, political, and social problems can ultimately be reduced to the human problem.

17

If we have learned anything in life, it is that the primary factor in everything is the person — the quality and spirit of the person.

18

It is those who are able to believe more, and keep greater hope in humanity's possibilities, who will be able to continue pushing humanity forward.

19

Progress requires the collaboration of the many, but it begins with the creative and innovative impulse of the few. It is, therefore, important that the many who collaborate be capable of overcoming the burdens of inertia and habit. This collaboration must be revitalized through the assimilation and circulation of the innovative energy of the few who are capable of seeing farther, and of discovering and applying new formulas.

20

People have tremendous energy. They need to be channeled, they need to be offered undertakings that are suitable and appealing to them, and the example of others who are convincing by how they live their lives.

21

People are the foundation of all things. As the people are, so will their society be. If people are just, upstanding, generous, noble, and honest, society will also be just, upstanding, generous, noble, and honest. What I mean is that society, the social sphere, is the best thermometer of the existence of true virtues in humanity.

22

23  First people, then cooperatives.

24  The interesting and key thing is not the cooperatives, but the cooperators. Likewise, it is not democracy, but democrats. Not so much ideas as life experiences.

25  Wherever there are people who are conscious of their dignity, who love freedom, who are resolved to meet the demands of social justice, and who are able to accept a regime of solidarity that benefits everyone equally, there is a basis for cooperativism, and optimal results can be expected.

26  Social formulas are only effective to the degree that those in whom they are embodied live up to them.

27  The human, the person (an intelligent, free, and responsible being), is the center and the axis of the cooperative structure and spirit.

28  What path are we on? Are we headed to advancement, or idiotic consumerism?

29  We aspire to economic development not as an end, but a means.

30  The cooperative ideal is to make people more human. If the main characteristic that distinguishes humans from animals is the quality of being rational and free, then becoming more human consists mainly of becoming more free, intelligent, conscious, and responsible, more nature's masters and less its slaves. Both misery and abundance can be forms of slavery when true courage and freedom of spirit are lacking.

People who cultivate their faculties with only production in mind, senselessly and fatally make themselves slaves of the productive machinery.

It is worthwhile to live and work for something beyond earning money and accumulating things for oneself. Community with others, peace, justice, understanding, sensitivity, and solidarity are things that have to be sought and achieved, and, to do that effectively in a world of struggle, one must think of another way to organize people who work and struggle.

For us, human beings are not a simple drop of water, destined to end up in the ocean, renouncing all efforts to maintain individuality and personality in pursuit of a series of human aspirations.

We must convince ourselves that true wealth lies in the integral development of our personality. Until we achieve that, even when we achieve distributive justice in the division of material goods, we will continue to be slaves.

Let us begin and end with people. People who better master nature, their own lives, and their rights and obligations, are, in the end, more human.

All the problems and issues in the world can definitively be reduced to people.

### 1.1.3 **Ideals**

37 Human rebellion is always invincible.

38 Humanity, which is too bent towards the ground, must again stand tall and look to the sky.

39 People suffocate when their only horizons are those that are temporary and limited.

40 What is a person? An imperfect being. A perfectable being. A being whose destiny is not to contemplate, but to transform. To transform oneself, and to transform everything around oneself.

41 We must act with our hearts, while still keeping our heads.

42 There is something fixed and eternal deep in the human spirit that needs to move towards a new and higher growth aligned with people's internal and social regeneration. So, people's social achievements must demonstrate this transformation.

43 The world has not been given to us simply to contemplate, but to transform, and this transformation is not made by hands, but first, with ideas and action plans.

44 Ideas do not die, and those who die faithful to their ideals usually give them new resonance and fertility.

45 When I hear music written by the hands of masters hundreds of years ago, when I see sculptures and paintings that are not forgotten despite the passage of years ...

When we still feel the influence of people who no longer exist, I believe that the people who created these marvels are still alive. When they reached the end of their journey, they rested in death ... without dying.

It is unquestionably preferable to be a wretched person than a well-fed pig; better to be a discontented Socrates, Paul, or Francis than a contented lunatic.

People who bend like reeds, who lack resolve, who are victims of the anguish of living, are incapable of building anything solid or firm.

Many who complain about their fate should only complain about themselves.

The saddest thing is not to admit one's mistakes, because if the mistake is analyzed with interest, and with dedication, some good can still be expected to come from it. The saddest thing is when we do not care about the truth, considering it to be a luxury good or a trivial matter.

People who are absorbed in solving external problems fail to remember that they have internal problems that are no less important. Their wellbeing, perhaps even their material welfare, depends more on the internal solutions than the external.

We carry within ourselves one who torments us in the name of God.

It is not a luxury, but a necessity, to live for the future more than for the present.

53 People need a long-range perspective and a longing for eternity to make their existence tolerable.

54 Great ideals do not necessarily have to be within reach to be useful.

55 Life is like a flavor or a perfume — once it dissipates, it cannot be re-concentrated or recovered. Will I not be careful how I invest it?

## 1.1.4 Man, Woman, Elder, Child

56 Our people suffer when only men are present.

57 The neighbors we always think of with interest, the strangers who come to weigh on our minds as much as or more than ourselves, are our children.

58 Our towns are being built without regard for the need for children's growth and recreation. We adults, however, will have our recreational centers, and even dazzling stadiums.

59 In our urban planning and developments, there are only posts to hang little signs: "No playing allowed."

60 Our children are often a birthright that we sell out for a dish of lentil stew.

61 In our society, there is still a notable lack of care or assistance options for children and the elderly. It is enough to

go out on the street on days off, or on school vacations, to see that the first obstacle is the fact that children are left to "hang out," because other than jail cells and classrooms, our society has not provided anything for them to enjoy doing with their leisure time safely or, better still, actively and educationally, which is to say, socially or communally. Their recreation centers have yet to be created.

We recognize human sensibility and refinement in two places, in children and the elderly, the two endpoints of life. 62

It is absurd how, overnight, active people in perfect health lose their authority, autonomy, and excitement for life, becoming people who are in the way, underestimated, owed nothing more than empty flattery and pampering. 63

NO TO RETIREMENT. 64

The weight of certain customs is great, and so it is that men, who are intelligent animals but firmly attached to their privilege, intentionally try to maintain their superiority. This is based on the exclusivity of power supported by skillfully formulated laws, to the point that men have insured their dominance for centuries with no special opposition, except during this or that age when it is said that matriarchy was dominant, but this was sporadic and without any great historical significance. 65

In every society, a woman's position is the exact measure of its level of development. 66

67  If women have little social consciousness, it is because our community has little social consciousness.

68  Women complain that they are disregarded and their capabilities and skills undervalued. That is true, but, in part, perhaps they should ask themselves: how much are we doing to put ourselves on equal terms? It is not enough to shed tears in the face of adverse luck; it is their duty to fight to conquer the position to which they are entitled, in good times and bad.

69  We men do not have the right, or it would be more precise to say that we do not have sufficient moral justification, to criticize women's behavior, when it is we who have organized society in such a manner that women have no other role than that of a puppet, of a lovely decorative object, whose sole end is to satisfy man, the king of society.

70  We men are victims of our own narrow-mindedness when we judge the capability and adaptability of women to engage in the widest variety of activities. Deep down, we rejoice in imagining our women as being infantile, and we see them through a prism of chronic weakness in the face of work and men. Perhaps a morbid feeling of superiority nests within us.

71  The greatest victories of science have served to redeem the most unredeemed of beings: women.

72  Encouraging women to flee domestic servitude seems as absurd to us as condemning them to it.

73  Men and women need each other, and they need each other in all spheres of human life and activity. Therefore,

trying to get ahead in life without the collaboration of women is like trying to run with only one foot.

Basque folk dance in Mondragón's Herriko Plaza, c. 1945.

# 1.2 Freedom

## 1.2.1 Freedom and Humanity

Humanity cannot flourish without freedom, and the bread we may obtain without freedom can only be bitter.

People well provided with or qualified for work are the warriors who will liberate and come to own our country. We work to win freedom for people and for our country because we need the right to live in justice and honesty.

There is no human ruler, no human power, capable of coming through the door to conquer or dominate my heart, whether with cleverness or with violence.

The first form of elemental justice that we need to practice is granting each other consideration as free beings.

Personal liberation is insecure as long as it does not focus on overcoming collective servitude.

Freedom is a heavy load that we can only carry with participatory training in all aspects of life.

80 Unity is compatible with diversity. The collective journey is, in reality, trial and error, an experimental search.

## 1.2.2 Freedom and Solidarity

81 With cooperation, we can act in solidarity, and in solidarity, we can make progress without masters, which is to say, with freedom and justice, and with social and economic emancipation.

82 We cannot speak of community where relationships and coexistence are based on the use of force.

83 We have gone from corrosive individualism to degrading collectivism.

84 Never has there been so much talk about freedom as during this century, and yet we have produced systems and theories that are the negation of all freedom. Never has there been so much talk of human value and dignity as in recent times, yet never before have people been respected less, looked down on more, sacrificed with so little care, or had their lives dismissed as so worthless. Never has there been so much talk as in recent years of humanity, the common good, shared class interests, the good of humanity — so many absurdities are justified with such pompous terms. We have reached a social situation in which, like never before in the world, the whims and ambition, pride and arrogance, and selfishness and cruelty of the strong are the order of the day. All this is

to the detriment of the true interests of the masses, the people, humanity. This is what we have come to.

Those who love freedom must not ignore that others crave it too. 85

Our country needs everyone's effort. Joining forces is not feasible in communities that have evolved without mutual respect, without freedom, and, as a consequence, without real and effective pluralism. 86

The cooperative experience, consistent with the profound democratic spirit of our country, and in an effective search for freedom—which the people have seen denied or bargained away many times and in many ways—has sought to pursue and secure this freedom and this wellbeing through the citizens' and workers' own efforts. 87

## 1.2.3 Freedom and Discipline

As the Dominican Lacordaire said, it is freedom that oppresses the weak, and law that sets the poor man free. 88

A driver on a highway or the streets of a modern city must be primarily concerned with obeying the traffic rules and with maintaining the speed imposed by the flow of traffic. Their safety and freedom depend on the degree of attention they pay to such laws and rules. A member of a worker cooperative is subject to laws and rules of organization and activity that are no less strict. 89

90   For the sake of that same freedom, we shun perfectionism and tolerate defects and inadequacies that could probably be overcome or remedied by more blunt and violent approaches. Is there any other way to overcome the temptation and risk of fundamentalism and totalitarianism?

91   One of the dominant features of the moral mindset that we need today must be tolerance, whose essential goal is the recognition of others.

92   Each person has within themselves a number of people, all of different opinions. Within the same person can be found a savant, an artist, a philosopher, a parent, a worker ... each with their own way of considering things, which is contrary to their neighbors.

93   Normally, inside each of us, there are various little characters waiting their turn to intervene and take vengeance. We all carry within us a camouflaged dictator, however much we may boast of being democrats. There is a selfish person within each of us, who is always ready to discover a selfish attitude in others, even when there is hardly any.

94   If we were able to conduct ourselves with more austerity in our individual lives, and knew how to transplant this same virtue into our social life, we could break many commitments, or at least not need to make so many.

95   The suppression of needs through self-discipline, penance, and fasting is the way to true freedom.

## 1.2.4 **Cooperative Democracy**

Dialogue and cooperation, freedom and commitment, all constitute effective methods for joining forces and efforts to organize and administer human labor, and thereby to humanize the economy. 96

Cooperative democracy must be operational and dynamic. Its greatest contribution is precisely that it pushes upward so that new values are advanced without interruption. 97

People get tired and worn out. Democracy is a source of renewal. 98

Our beloved democracy can degenerate into dictatorship through the abuse of power by those on top, or the abdication of power by those at the bottom. 99

Where are we going, when those who must command only partially know how to do so, or when those who should obey do so with reservations, at their discretion, so as to run away from some imaginary oppression or exploitation? Being free is not a luxury, but a necessity and a duty. 100

Democracy, once nobly adopted, is conducive to discipline, to responsibility, to the deepening of solidarity. In short, democracy is conducive to authentic social progress. 101

Democracy must help us find balance. 102

Housing developed in the early 1950s through the Asociación Mondragonesa del Hogar, founded by Arizmendiarrieta.

# 1.3 Responsibility

## 1.3.1 Responsibility and Self-Management

The self-managed society will be the one that we all, with our preparation and willingness to participate, will be able to bring about.  103

It has been said that a person who needs a master is an animal. As soon as they become a real human being, this need disappears.  104

But at times, one gets to thinking that all these efforts to tell us that things are complex, and that we do not understand them, is a cover for a desire to leave the world the way it is, which we workers do not like.  105

We workers have clear ideas. We do not like people who self-identify as undisputed leaders, or are declared to be so by cliques with a stake in their power.  106

Someone once said that the mature person is the one who, after losing their dreams, holds on to THE DREAM. We would add that the mature person is the one  107 who — between the past, where memories linger, and the future, where dreams can be found — is with the present, where RESPONSIBILITIES are.

108 Between the past, where our memories lie, and the future, where we keep our dreams, we must face the present, embracing the duties imposed on us by our circumstances.

109 Let us not brag of being mature and progressive people unless each and every one of us acts with due reflection and seriousness. How many of the things that we've felt satisfied with and even proud of at one time or another have we really taken seriously?

110 Having a sense of responsibility means no more and no less than considering oneself totally irreplaceable for the task with which one has been entrusted.

111 Circumstances, it has been said, are neither good nor bad, they are what each of us want them to be. Opportunities exist for those who decide to take them.

112 Reason is the powerful resource that people use to satisfy their needs and pursue their goals. Through foresight and then planning, people join the present to the future, prioritize their needs, and make appropriate use of their strengths.

113 There is no harvest without sowing, nor is anything produced by spontaneous generation. It is not noble to ask others for that which we are able to provide or do for ourselves.

114 This cooperative experience has demonstrated that

workers are mature enough to undertake endeavors with a broad social impact. Perhaps the same could not be said of the sectors of our population who enjoy above-average educational or economic status.

## 1.3.2 Responsibility and Solidarity

Individuals and families for the rich, and social institutions for the poor. There is a name for this: social underdevelopment. <sup>115</sup>

We are trying to see that the much-vaunted socialization will be possible when we see to it that the staircase to our building, which belongs to several neighbors, is cared for as well as our apartment, and that our children go to the schools and colleges of the less powerful. We will try to equip our children well for this, so there will be authentic equality of opportunity, and to invest the money we could have spent on a luxurious bathroom on a rational water system instead, so that the whole population will be better served. <sup>116</sup>

No one who is in need should be left unprotected, but nor should protection be provided indiscriminately without differentiating between those who conduct themselves with diligence and foresight and those who are careless about things that should not be neglected. <sup>117</sup>

One cannot sit at another's table indefinitely without contributing anything. Everyone benefits from society, and so must return the favor, and offer service. <sup>118</sup>

119 We will be on the right path when no one in our ranks is left behind, but also not too many are carried through the effort of others.

120 No one is useless, only misused.

121 Nothing reveals the extent of a person's true personality like their propensity for, or submission to, respect for people.

122 There are silences that are betrayals; silences that imply complicity.

123 In the face of good and evil, or justice and injustice, there can be no hesitation.

124 An easy temptation for many workers, whose whole mindset has been shaped by the need to unite around demands on the employer, is to avoid taking personal responsibility for the economic process that all development entails, especially cooperative development.

125 At the base of a healthy cooperativism, we must have people who have a profound sense of responsibility, who are personally involved in the economic process, and who are subject to social pressure from their respective communities.

126 So far, our contribution to the people has consisted of this cooperative experience; from now on, we should offer community development characterized by foresight and coherence.

127 In a cooperative, we are all responsible for everything.

Ceremony of blessing for banners of the international lay society Catholic Action, 1942.

# 1.4
# Morals

## 1.4.1 Human Maturity

For us to be a mature people, a collective of adults, we need to assign greater value to the state of consciousness that governs our relationships and mutual harmony than to signs of opulence and vain prestige. 128

Individual moral formation must continue to be the foundation of social education. 129

The most effective way to assure the common good is to pursue selfless personal perfection. The better the artist, the better the symphony. 130

We need resilient people, not pampered children. People who feel deep in their consciences the call of a hopeful working world. Activists in the cause of freedom and of justice, neither indifferent nor passive about the new world that must be built. 131

The builders of humanity in its grandeur are, above all, the few who consecrate their lives to spiritual and moral values. 132

133 There is a virtue called generosity, and a quality called good will, which, when they guide our actions, are all we need to solve even the most difficult problems.

134 Without the generous gifts of the people, sacrificing their selfish appetites, great works could neve be done.

135 Knowing how to control oneself, and do so effectively, is as necessary to social life as wings are to a bird in flight.

136 The selfish and the individualistic are the fifth column of cooperation.

137 What a shame that good old Pythagoras is not alive today! Instead of his unnecessary theorem about the square of the hypotenuse and the sides, I am sure he would have shown that the square of the penalty area of the rival team is equal to the total penalty area of the home team plus the sum of the square meters occupied by the fans, multiplied by the volume of their shouts. If anyone doubts this, ask the referees.

138 Truths and laws, whether mathematical, moral, or social, imply a servitude that brings nothing but benefit to those who recognize them with all their consequences.

139 Focused attention, character formation, self-control, technical education, moral vigor, and social conscience all need to be carefully tended if one wishes to maintain internal balance and avoid being dragged through life, lost and undifferentiated, like a drop of water in a river on its way to the sea.

140 Before we dream of making leaders, we have to think about making people. Before teaching them public rela-

tions and manners, we have to get them used to forgetting about themselves.

141 Without moral law, neither individuals nor peoples can avoid decadence or maintain their material possessions. Peoples without conscience always fall into abject barbarism, in which even the order and harmony that instinct engenders in the unreasonable disappears.

142 The vigor and bravery of instinct, legendary as they may be, do nothing to make up for failings nor do they offer a remedy for powerlessness.

143 The person dominated by the instinct to win is no more than a product of nature, condemned as such to be like wheat, a cow, or a fruit tree — abandoned to fate and nature's laws.

144 Cooperative efforts at transformation don't know their own worth or value themselves exclusively on the basis of their economic results, and only rarely for what they mean for human and social training and maturity. It may be that we cooperators ourselves, leaders as well as members, are the least capable of assessing what is most valuable and definitive in our own experience.

145 The idea of "having more" bewitches us and greatly devalues our life by focusing it on "having more" and the corresponding status symbols.

146 Progress is not acquiring more, but being more, behaving better, giving more of oneself.

147 "To act and not to win, to create and not to possess, to progress and not to dominate."

148   The good thing that is not developed will come to an end, just as uncultivated nature ends up yielding less of its bounty.

149   Human values are drawn only from fidelity to the human conscience.

150   These days, we are used to blaming everything on institutions and on social and political structures, and we've come to expect that the rise of new political and social institutions will solve everything. I am not trying to say that all institutions and social and political structures are equally good or bad. Rather, I mean that they are of secondary importance, if we think about it carefully, because the source of good or evil, the principal source of good or evil, is within people, who are not transformed by external factors. People's dignity, honesty, and righteousness come only from their own hearts, and from loyalty to their conscience. And we do not want to talk about that, we do not want to think about that. The worst misfortune for human beings is not that they suffer under this or that political or social regime, but that their moral sense has disappeared and their conscience carries no weight. A community that has lost its moral sense and its conscience can not fight against its problems nor alleviate them except with the abuse of force, which, in turn, degrades and bestializes people even more.

151   People must recognize their limitations, their dependence, they must recognize the hierarchy of values, the primacy of reason over instinct, and the existence of a natural law that connects everything in nature and themselves as part of it.

## 1.4.2 **Christianity**

To believe in the Gospel is to believe in people, in their vocation and dignity, more than in their lineage or culture, their wealth or their power. 152

The proclamation of the rights of Jesus Christ is the affirmation of the rights of the powerless. 153

The great truths, if such they are, and by simply being so, are understandable by all. 154

Conscience is more than a conventional rule, it is the voice of humanity and of God. 155

Truly, we must pity a person, especially a modern person, whose personal and conscious life has been reduced to a bare minimum. 156

The duty to be good is more urgent than the right to be happy. 157

People have such a strong and vivid feeling of the excellence of virtue that even the greatest crimes are disguised under its cloak. 158

Who would dare to justify everything that has been done in the name of humanity, order, society, the Republic, or God, in these past years? 159

Injustice, revenge, hatred, hunger... how can God tolerate all this? 160

161 Teaching only the proper way for people to behave with one another, without confronting their selfishness, is like plowing the sea.

162 What we Christians have thrown in our faces, and not without reason, is that we preach one doctrine and practice another.

163 To be a Christian is not only to possess the truth, but, above all, to practice the truth, which is the same as doing good.

164 If being a Christian were nothing more than possessing the truth, and if it were enough for Christians to embrace it, then even a phonograph record could be a Christian.

165 The good idea, the right word, is the one that becomes action.

166 We appreciate the true dimension of a person by measuring their heart, not their cleverness or the scope of their intelligence.

167 Love is the indispensable complement of justice.

168 Charity must be the complement of justice. Those who do not feel this, and practice it, can be considered traffickers of feelings that human beings cannot sell.

169 Fortunate is the community for whom the Church is a friend, because that Church will have magnificent resources with which to protect its rights and safeguard its dignity. No one will ever be able to tyrannize the community that has the Church at its side.

The technical college, an early initiative of Arizmendiarrieta, in its first home, 1943–51.

# 1.5 Education

## 1.5.1 Culture and Personality

A person becomes a person more through education than through birth. 170

Only through education can a person become a person. 171

A person is not so much born as made through education. 172

It's not just by being born that we become people, but by virtue of an educational process in the broadest sense of the term; through knowledge and experience. 173

People become human through education. Civilization progresses rapidly through training or education oriented by the search for human and social values. 174

Human nature is not simply nature, but an artifice, which is to say, nature transformed, adapted, or developed by work and technique. 175

In a wild forest, the strength and vigor of the earth are squandered just as much on the sap that makes a fruit 176

177 Education is economics, because without education, scarce goods and services cannot be produced nor distributed.

178 It is easier to educate a young person than to reform an adult.

179 Teaching must be ongoing to be effective.

180 Tools and machines need to be checked and repaired, but above all, we need to renew the mindset of the people who are destined to exercise dominion over these elements.

181 Culture is the blood that always gives people heritage and nobility.

182 The only heritage and value that does not tend to lose its value is the empowerment of people: learning.

183 Intelligence is the unshakeable foundation of equality that God has placed in all people.

### 1.5.2 Culture and Emancipation

184 Knowledge is power.

185 Knowledge must be socialized to democratize power.

The socialization of culture is inevitably followed by the socialization of wealth and even of power. We could even say that this is the indispensable condition for democratization and the socioeconomic progress of a people. 186

Let us not forget that it was when the bourgeoisie reached a higher level of education that it overpowered and dethroned the aristocracy, and that, therefore, the proletariat will only be in a position to begin its social reign when it has the necessary technical and cultural capacity and preparation to replace or relieve the bourgeoisie. 187

The transformation and cultivation of people through education is an unavoidable presupposition in every situation and every case in every social structure. 188

The most active agents of renewal are education, science, and technology, which have a common denominator: people with a new mindset. 189

Education, understood as the complex of ideas and conceptions that a person adopts, is the key to the development and unfolding of a people. 190

Education is the natural and indispensable fulcrum for the promotion of a new social order that is just and humane. 191

We should be concerned with the underdeveloped areas that can be found anywhere, but especially the ones under our caps and berets. ... Openness and forward thinking are the imperatives of the present hour, in all aspects of life and human relations. A radical change in mindset is the order of the day. 192

193 Knowledge is power, and to democratize power, knowledge must first be socialized. We accomplish nothing by proclaiming rights if the people whose rights we have proclaimed are incapable of administering those rights, or if, to be able to act, they have no other option but to depend on a few irreplaceable individuals.

194 The emancipation of a class or of a people must begin with the mass empowerment of its individual members. The fate of the masses is not improved without the masses.

195 Again and again we say that we must fight against social injustices, against the exploitation of the wage worker, against the excessive accumulation of wealth, etc., etc., but have we understood that the principal servitude, the first and most dire slavery, is intellectual poverty?

196 The saddest inheritance left to us by the world that came before is undoubtedly the lack of opportunities for education and training, not economic inequality.

197 The young person who plunges into the world of work today without a clear and positive social ideology is either a castaway from their religious life, or a coward and a traitor to the workers' movement.

198 We believe that more than a lack of imagination, we are hobbled by special interests and the inertia of a precarious culture. The former esconces the powerful and influential, while the latter keeps the masses numb to the real causes of our discomfort and lack of possibilities.

199 When education is the privilege of one social class, communities are unable to progress, resulting in a servitude

that is at once anti-economic and anti-social. Those people and communities who grasp this truth without much difficulty try at all costs to spread and socialize education. The socialization of education, access to it without discrimination, and the granting of opportunities for self-improvement to all people to the limits of their potential are fundamental tenets of every contemporary social movement. Proclamations of human rights made without corresponding economic and educational support are ephemeral concessions made for show, and are destined to have no lasting effect.

We know the longing for freedom of the poor, of the proletarians — in a word, of the people. This longing is good, and reflects well on the people, on their sense of dignity, which, as we all know, has one watchword: freedom. How sad to realize that these longings cannot be satisfied, even in the best of cases, since those who feel them are not capable of managing their own interests and rights, because they lack the preparation and skill to do so, because they lack knowledge. People who love freedom, people who know their rights, must know that freedom can not be possessed by people who are unable to take responsibility, people who live out their lives as minors. Such people must concern themselves with education, because the path of illiteracy and ignorance can only lead to slavery, even if it is called something else. 200

Teaching is an indispensable element for the true emancipation of the worker. 201

A person or a people who are conscious of their dignity, or who do not want to live at the expense of others or outsiders, must, above all, focus above all on the cultivation and development of their own intelligence and willpower. 202

203   Making the most of our people's talents, without regard to their personal or family economic condition, is a fundamental premise of all social action aimed at the constitution of a more humane, more Christian, social order.

204   The redistribution of wealth is necessary, but the socialization of education is more pressing, to be able to think about the true humanization of work.

205   A foolish person does more damage than a wicked one, because the wicked occasionally rest, but the fool never does.

206   The "underdeveloped" zones we most need to attend to are our own heads.

207   The most fruitful and profitable planning is that applied to the development of people, upon whom healthy communities can be raised and established.

208   The best way to make a dynamic community in which initiatives of all kinds can flourish is by giving a broad range of options to everyone who is in a position to cultivate their higher faculties.

209   Education is the key to the fate and future of our young people and of our society itself.

210   Under no circumstances can we dream of a better tomorrow if we do not concern ourselves with preparing it, specifically by shaping the tender souls of those who will soon be tomorrow's men and women.

Children are our glory or our ruin, and whether they become one or the other depends on the outcome of the educational activity we do.

211

Our fate depends more on the classrooms through which we have passed than the cribs into which we were born.

212

Plants take time to sink their roots deep into the earth. The same can be said of feelings and ideas in the spirits of people and communities, the only difference being that the latter takes even longer than the former. That is because, while the lives of plants are measured in decades or centuries, the history of humanity is usually counted in millennia.

213

The formation of a person begins a hundred years before their birth.

214

To change the constitution of a nation, or the form or administration of a government is something that can be done overnight. The same goes for changing a law. Putting someone new in charge is relatively easy. It takes no time at all. But no one doubts that changing a beast into a person, perfecting oneself even a bit, and controlling and overcoming the evil inclinations that arise within us all, take time and effort. Improvisation will not work.

215

Teaching and education are the primary undertakings of a community.

216

### 1.5.3 Education and Cooperativism

217 Education and cooperation are linked in much the same way as work and the worker whose self-realization is accomplished individually and collectively, overcoming the inertia of individuals' original nature and status.

218 It has been said that cooperativism is an economic movement that makes use of educational action, but we can just as well affirm that it is an educational movement that makes use of economic action.

219 Education, as a didactic and existential process, must involve consciousness raising about, and practice of, work.

220 Work and study must go hand in hand. We must never disregard the possibilities of those who work, nor underestimate work options for those who stall out in their studies, or grow tired of them. If we want our communities to be seamless, we must provide equality of opportunity continuously throughout life.

221 Democracy and inherited privileges do not mix.

222 The merits of the principle of educational opportunity must be married to the requirements of equitable distribution of the burdens necessary for its realization.

223 Let us combine WORK and CULTURE, and let us keep them linked together in the service of a progressive community, for the good of humanity.

224 Cooperative enterprises have to avoid immobility at all costs, by constantly fine-tuning their people, attentively

assessing their skills, and systematically updating or adjusting them.

The implementation of financial plans must be monitored as carefully as the implementation of methods for human development, so that people's potential is applied under the best conditions. Education and training are much more profitable than positive balances or returns on investment. 225

Education amounts to the cultivation of all human virtues, among which the ability to think stands out especially. 226

Ideas and the mindset they entail and promote are no less indispensable to the proper functioning of our cooperatives than their facilities and machines. 227

Ulgor, first of Mondragón's industrial worker-cooperatives, with foundry under construction in 1957.

# 1.6
# The Sign of Vitality

## 1.6.1 "There Is Always One More Step to Take"

There is always one more step to take. 228

The sign of vitality is not to endure, but to be reborn and to adapt. 229

Development is our great goal, because deep down, people live on hope. 230

Not regrets, but action. Don't mourn, act. 231

The future belongs to people who, in each moment and every generation, are able to grow and change, refusing to live off other people's money, and instead supporting themselves through their own virtue and capacity. 232

How many habits of an outmoded or outdated bourgeoisie are we reviving? We presume ourselves to be progressives, but are we turning out to be conservatives and traditionalists of the very worst kind? 233

234 Life rolls over those who do not progress.

235 The world has not been given to us to contemplate, but to transform.

236 To live is to struggle, whether we like it or not. This is because learning requires struggle, gaining new skills requires struggle, loving requires struggle, and we must struggle to be something.

237 People are creatures who have found nothing on earth that suits them. But, at the same time, they have the power to make use of everything, subjecting it to the dominion of their reason and ordering it to satisfy their needs. So we have no reason to complain about our fate. If we want, we can be sovereigns and architects of an order that accommodates and satisfies us.

238 Doctrine that is not put into practice, convictions that are not translated into acts, are as abnormal as a heart that does not beat, movement that does not vibrate. We were not placed on this earth to contemplate or complain about it, but to transform it.

239 Usually the worst impediments to development lie in the realm of the spirit.

240 The most difficult thing to justify is the absence of a desire to improve.

241 It is better to make a mistake than to do nothing. Besides, by making mistakes, you learn to get it right.

242 Nature responds splendidly to our demands when we know how to approach it, transform it, and nurture it

with our work. The material universe is malleable matter, which can be domesticated to serve people. It is inexhaustible, because matter extends over millions of light-years, and each gram contains billions of electron-volts.

Cooperativism tends toward order which is not static, but is in constant evolution towards a better form. It is equilibrium in motion. An inert action is a contradiction, and cooperativism, which was born from action and experience, rather than theory, is something that we must conceive of and desire in the constant search for better forms of expression. 243

We must improve ourselves. The struggle to transform what we find unsatisfactory is indispensable, whether the weakness is in our organization or our vision of, and commitment to, the future. 244

We must constantly and progressively revise our positions and banish fatigue by maintaining a process of unification, permeated by a new spirit. 245

A person or a community without the will to improve does not constitute a fertile field for cultivation of worker cooperatives. 246

## 1.6.2 Cooperativism Is an Experience

Cooperativism is not something we should live out as if what is accepted and settled at a given moment were unchangeable. Rather, we should be open to it as an exper- 247 imental process in which modifications that contribute to updating the means can and should be adopted, while safeguarding the nobility and worthiness of the high ends being pursued. Our own personal evolution and the evolution determined by everything around us, our relationships and coexistence with others, the degree of integrity, seriousness, responsibility, and initiative consolidated through organizational arrangements and experience itself, are new factors that can prompt us to once again review everything about the organization, to better serve the humanist goals we have set.

248   Feeling satisfied is an intolerable luxury. It is an attitude that those who wish to live decently cannot square with the human and social conscience within them. Those who enjoy certain privileges must think of contributions they can make to encourage and coordinate a process of continuous development, for themselves and for others.

249   The thing is, neither collective nor communitarian ownership by workers nor a framework of solidarity are enough in themselves to put an end to anguish and suffering. Those pains persist, and will continue to persist, as long as people embrace new means of self-realization and reach for new milestones. Perhaps, at some point, it will become clear to those who once thought that the cooperative solution would solve everything (as one might well imagine) how unrealistic those assumptions are, and they will be able to avoid needless dissatisfaction.

250   We make no apologies for limitations that others may point out. We are on the move. We appreciate those who make us aware of our defects and even our lack of fidelity to the principles that we have embraced. However weak or powerless we may seem to them, we remain faithful to

the cause of work and social justice, and we ask them to help us.

The Stone Age, which has been left far behind in the material realm, lives on in our spirit and social mentality. 251

It is curious to think that the best part of victory may be the struggle. 252

Good people working with bad instruments can rarely do anything well, and the most regrettable and damaging thing to the community is not bad people using good instruments to do evil, but good people whose bad instruments condemn them to work badly. These instruments are nothing other than institutions and the structures that make up those institutions. 253

The key to development, as well as to the coexistence and activity of our people, is its population and the spirit that has enlivened it. 254

Trust in the virtues of our people and the will of our communities to overcome, forged both in the tenacious struggle with nature and in other setbacks that may have touched their souls. We must not only be able to recover, but also to progress without dominating, and for that, today, with the help of the Caja Laboral Popular, we must endeavor to create and act. 255

An EXPERIENCE that tries to be a vital, expansive process, inspired by the human and social values born of the active conscience of our people and communities, needs to assimilate data relevant to this public conscience. Rather than a pretext to postpone transformation, it should be a mechanism of anticipation and acceleration. 256

257  If the sign of vitality is, in the end, not to endure, but to be reborn, as a great cooperativist rightly said, if cooperativism is not only the polar opposite of paternalism, but also of conformity and conservatism, and is not tied to any dogmatism, then we need to take our place in the vanguard of social innovations, especially when these are demanded by an awareness of dignity and freedom, of justice and solidarity. Those who share these feelings today do not lack strength. Their strength is enormous, because these feelings drive all noble spirits. It is our belief that the majority of people are sensible, that is, sensitive to great ideals.

258  Renew or die. The sign of vitality is not to endure but to change, and to try to anticipate the future. Research is a precondition for this.

259  The best indicator of the authentic vitality of a people is their will to improve themselves and actively participate in the solution to shared problems.

260  The most universal and appropriate activity for societies or communities that would not resign themselves to falling behind is research. Today, or soon, doing research is not a whim or a luxury, but a vital necessity, something all those who would not live at the expense of others must face up to and undertake.

261  To live is to walk and walk without being able to turn back. At every stage of life, people find themselves facing new difficulties and problems, which are impossible to avoid by retreating, and they must overcome them, or else risk succumbing to them. It is this historical law that regulates the march of humanity.

262 We are on the right path and determined not to stop pursuing any goal as long as freedom and justice require our collaboration.

# 2 Work and the Cooperative Enterprise

Arizmendiarrieta and workers, 1940s.

# 2.1
# Work

## 2.1.1 The Dignity of Work

Work is, above all, a service to the community and a way of developing the person. 263

Work is not a punishment from God, but proof of God's trust in people, making them his collaborators. 264

Regrettably, insistence on the fatal consequences of original sin has been pressed to the point of erasing any glimmer of reason. People, caught in the grip of tradition, were slow to discover the intimate nature of their potential, and, more importantly, the value of their own dignity as collaborators with God in the task of completing his unfinished work: nature. 265

In other words, God makes people members of his enterprise, of the marvelous enterprise that is creation. People, through their activity, transform and multiply things. 266

Work, for us, will never be a punishment and idleness a blessing from heaven, nor can wealth be the proper 267 path to human paradise. For us, work is the human contribution to the divine plan and designs to transform and improve a world which, while it may not become an earthly paradise, should still aspire to become more comfortable than it is today.

268   Here, it will not be out of place to reproduce the text sculpted on stone in one of the manor houses of Mondragon, that of the Artazubiagas, better known as the Center. Under a shield decorated with a lighted torch held in a hand and bordered with the text "pro libertate combusta," the lintel of the front door reads: "Solus labor parit virtutem et virtus parit honorem." Those of us who do not know much Latin and are in a hurry to finish this commentary will translate it by saying that "where there is no effort, there is no virtue, nor honor without virtue." That is, the lazy and idle may not use these doors, because there is also another one that reads: "through this door only works pass."

269   Economic development represents human progress and constitutes a true moral duty. In the eyes of a believer, underemployment, in all of its forms, is a scandal.

270   Our people are aware that their level of well-being and strength has come from the work potential of their children. These reserves and contingents of workers have been the armies spreading our historic personality, for which we are known in the world.

271   Work is the characteristic expression of the human species. Work is interpreted as intelligent action on nature, transforming it into a good, into something useful.

Through their work people transform nature and make it fertile, and work is the best legacy a community possesses. 272

Work may be very meritorious, but when the work is later spoiled or goes up in smoke, it cannot be said that it received the treatment it deserves. 273

To live with dignity, one must embrace work. 274

The need and opportunity to resort to and count on one's own resources or personal capabilities has led many more people to success than have any paternalistic catapults. It is not uncommon for the second-born to shine much brighter than the first-born heirs to the family fortune. 275

Work is the attribute that awards us the highest honor of being a cooperator with God in the transformation and cultivation of nature and in the consequent advancement of human welfare. The fact that people exercise their faculty of work in union with their peers and in a structure of noble cooperation and solidarity gives them not only nobility, but also the optimal productivity to make every corner of the earth a pleasant and promising mansion for all. This is what work communities are for, and they are destined to help our people advance. 276

Work is a path of personal and communal self-realization, individual perfection, and collective improvement; it is the epitome of an unquestionable social and humanist consciousness. 277

Communities do not become wealthy by winning the lottery. 278

## 2.1.2 Humanizing Work

279 The future is for those who know how to work and to ennoble work.

280 Is not labor a nobler, older, and more human element than capital, and as such, worthy of greater esteem? Is it an unjustifiable ambition for its representatives to claim primacy in leadership?

281 Justice is the virtue that commands that each be given their own. Cooperativism renders unto labor that which is labor's and unto capital that which is capital's.

282 People and communities that have been most pampered by nature are not necessarily those who shine the brightest in history.

283 To continue enjoying well-being, just as to be free, we must prepare ourselves to work better, in better human and social conditions and with products and surpluses that are more universally desirable for their quality or suitability for the advancement of all their recipients.

284 To work well is to make something well-made and made in a good way. It is not a tautology. A well-made thing, in other words, is something useful, which fills a need, whose cost is less than its price, and whose price is fair and accepted. A thing made in a good way, with technique, organization, and collaboration, is the product of a unity of voluntary efforts. The worker is always respected, because the ends never, ever, justify the means, and people, whether their status is high or low, are always the most important thing.

Charity is to work well. 285

The best way for humanity to live better is to produce more and better, which is to say, to increase the two basic factors: productivity and quality. 286

I believe that assigning positions to capable women, in the same way, and with the same determination, that we assign positions to men, is a social objective and an issue that concerns us all. It does not seem right, by definition, to deny that to which all of us have a right and obligation: to work, and to do so with maximum performance. 287

The value of work is independent of gender. 288

The sign of maturity is participation and integration into the collective endeavor. 289

The worker who does not find the satisfaction that demanded by sensibilities and natural capacities in their work is a worker who will inevitably sow dissatisfaction around them. 290

The problem of our day is not how to find a way to escape work, but instead how to make work a service, and, where possible, a source of honest satisfaction. Work can and should be humanized. 291

Arizmendiarrieta and folk dancers, 1940s.

# 2.2 Unity

## 2.2.1 Human Foundation

We should begin by considering all people citizens of equal dignity and destiny.     292

The destiny of each is linked to that of the rest.     293

Plants and people can defend themselves better when cultivated and supported in groups.     294

People and communities, just like flowers and other species of beings, survive and triumph in groups, not in isolation.     295

People fulfill their role as rulers of creation to the extent that they subordinate their own accomplishments to that which is everlasting inside them. Realizing oneself means reaching out to, and relying on, one's peers.     296

It is often said that there is no manifestation of force or power in the cosmos without repercussion and reciprocity, nor a cry that fades without an echo. The only exception is a heart that is unmoved by the pain     297 of others. A person with such a heart is a monster that does not even belong to the category of human, much less Christian.

298 We are all more indebted to others than we imagine.

299 We cannot claim to be civil or just if we forget all that we have received from the community and from the generations that have preceded us, and if we do not make adequate contributions in return.

300 Today the individual, the person, signifies so little that to preserve their personality, they need to be immersed into, and to a certain extent even conflated with, the group. A drop of water that wants to preserve its personality must lose itself in the ocean, because if it does not, it will evaporate and disappear. Likewise, the individual and the person need the help and support of others.

301 People, apart from their personal baggage, which has been molded in the family home, forge their personalities in a continuous process of integration by accepting or rejecting concepts and situations the environment presents them.

302 No doubt the most hopeful sign for a group is to know how to unite to build, to construct what matters now and for the future.

303 To contemplate a person in the context of their community is to see them clothed in the benevolence and support of their peers.

304 The formula for the person who wants to succeed: Don't struggle alone.

Having faith in solidarity is precisely this: to believe in others as we believe in ourselves, and to expect of others what we expect of ourselves. 305

We come together to do what is right, and we take the path of solidarity to advance towards freedom. 306

## 2.2.2 Economic Foundation

We have neither been aligned with nor will we resign ourselves to aligning with the pursuit of ideas that clash with reality. Given the choice between ideas that divide us and a reality that leads us to unite and coexist, we choose the latter, and it is because of this that we repudiate so much ideology as being simple utopianism. 307

Is there anything the working world requires right now more than unity? And, can unity be considered better than trying to identify ourselves with values that, in themselves, are universal? 308

The best known trait of Basque people the world over is their yearning for freedom. Let us feed that desire now with the spirit of integrity, and work and solidarity will bring progress to our people. 309

The economic system looks more and more like a clock. If one part does not work, the clock tends to stop. 310

In reality, we are all in solidarity; it is not necessary to belong to the same cooperative enterprise for this. The 311 economy is structured more and more on the basis of a growing division of labor. Everything is done by everyone. The agricultural, industrial, and service sectors are members of a community, of a single economic process. It is, therefore, a question of becoming aware of this basic solidarity, of being attuned to it in its many aspects.

312 The workers in a company will be able to assert their position as the labor factor at the heart of the company as long as they have representation and an active role. The community of labor needs to have a legal entity.

313 Humanity today is condemned to the persistence of restricted castes and antagonistic classes, depriving us of solidarity and fellowship, due to economic inequalities reinforced by privilege and denial of access to opportunities for culture and education.

314 Where there is equality, fellowship and solidarity reign. When this base is lacking, these feelings are usually ephemeral.

315 Overcoming individual servitude can only be achieved by consolidating community structures with broad social bases.

316 Let us help each other and be certain that others will help us, and together we will make our way.

317 Isolated workers are indeed weak, but united, they are a first-rate power. They must be summoned to a new effort to secure total social emancipation on the firm foundation of adequate economic structures.

We live infected by the sin of a suicide and a homicide of global proportions.

## 2.2.3 **Solidarity**

For me, it is the key and even, if you like, the atomic secret, called to revolutionize all social life: class collaboration, collaboration of the people with their authorities and of the authorities with their people, collaboration of theory and spirit. This is the secret of an authentic social life and the key to social peace. It is not enough for the bosses to do good works, the workers must participate in them; it is not enough for the workers to dream of great reforms, the bosses must participate in them; it is not enough for the authorities to work hard and go to great lengths, the people must be with them. Where the authorities are divorced from the people, where the bosses follow a path without incorporating the workers into it, no spontaneous social life is possible. Any peace will be fictitious, and at any moment, the deception may turn into surprise and shock.

Collaboration in everything, so that everything is the fruit of the effort and sacrifice of all, and the glory, too, is shared.

The communities that triumph are those that apply themselves best, accelerating their progress by building unity.

322  Let us form a community that is convinced of being one, and its power will be immense. Let us collaborate with all without discrimination, as long as they are people of good will.

323  Unity is the strength of the weak. Solidarity is the mighty lever that multiplies our strength.

324  At the moment, what is most needed by our community is the strength derived from the union of its people, its labor, and its inhabitants. And all this can be combined in the advancement and support of the force of reason without renouncing the reason of force. In this way, we will ensure that truth and justice are at the service of freedom and the well-being of all.

325  If we wish to be practical and consequential people, let us work for the reign of justice and good, no matter who agrees with us in this undertaking.

326  Being in solidarity means accepting our peers, not just as they are, but also as they should be; tolerating their limitations and defects, without giving up the good impulse that leads us to embrace them in the hope that through our service they will improve themselves. Freedom and solidarity cannot be opposing or exclusive values, but rather, complementary. Our dedication and contribution must be so spontaneous and natural as to lead to the transformation of our own inherited human nature, which can be a bit petty, as well as that of our peers, our neighbors, who are the agents of their own transformation.

327  Human coexistence happens to the extent that people know how to accept each other just as they are, with each one's nature and idiosyncrasies.

If we wish to count on others, we must begin by seriously counting on ourselves. It is essential that we begin the process of solidarity by each of us relying more on personal reflection, drawing on a critical, objective sense. This is not some tactful recommendation that we leave our heart aside, but simply that we should always keep the heart where it belongs in any well-formed person: below the head.

Collectives that enjoy authentic peace and well-being are those in which each member pursues his or her own good by uniting it with the interests of others.

Solidarity is not some purely theoretical proclamation, but something that must be put into action and made manifest by willingly accepting the restrictions of teamwork and association, since this is the way we can help one another.

The right to private property is good to the extent that it serves to maintain the freedom of its owner, but must in no way trample on, limit, or deprive others of their freedom. Thus, we must use what is ours to do what best suits us as individuals, understanding this within the community in which we live, because if we fail to take this into account, we could do harm to others.

Ownership does not grant the owner the right to abuse goods. In the final analysis, none of us can rightly feel that our role in their creation of our goods gives us an absolute right to dispose of them. Many people have played a part in their existence and production, and the common good must be weighed and taken into account in their use and practical application.

333 Practicing solidarity once in a while, or simply at one's discretion, is not enough to transform it into an authentic force and human value. That is a broken lever.

334 None of our acts is irrelevant, all have some social repercussion.

335 Not long ago, the sage worked alone. Pasteur and Curie were isolated, or teachers with a few disciples around them. Today, there is only teamwork.

336 We know that one link is not the chain, but a chain becomes useless if one link is broken.

337 It is what we contribute to the commons that demonstrates the authenticity of our feeling of solidarity, not what we require or seek from it as an institution.

338 We need to pay as much attention, or more, to communal rights as to individual rights.

339 Those who, with a consciousness of solidarity, have accepted their membership in a cooperative workforce know that effective solidarity exists to the extent that each one knows how to give up what is theirs for the sake of the common good.

340 In both theory and in practice, solidarity is the constant element in the cooperative equation.

341 Our strength does not translate into struggle, but rather, cooperation.

342 Good cooperative enterprises are made up of people who are capable of bearing witness to solidarity and the de-

sire to improve by putting their personal assets or their personal credit on the line.

Not in solitude, but in solidarity. 343

To the extent that I give myself over to it, communal passion, passion for the collective advancement of humanity, will make me see that the agricultural sector is, in many aspects, a weaker sector than industry, and I will be driven to show my solidarity with it in various ways. 344

Workers and farmers who make a living from their work must move forward in mutual solidarity so they can become strong in the common struggle for their interests. 345

We cannot imagine a healthy industrial development if our family farms, our agricultural sector, do not have the same level of development as other sectors. Progress has to be shared and harmonious. The saying "every man for himself and the devil take the hindmost" is worthless. If one sector fails, the rest will seize up. 346

Divide and conquer. The divisions within the workers movement have been a great misfortune. But neither should we forget what history and our own experience teach us: hopeful struggles have failed due to a lack of solidarity between industrial workers and farmers, their failure to combine in a united front. 347

Solidarity and honesty are inherently profitable. 348

Basque combatants and priest during Spain's Civil War, 1937. Arizmendiarrieta in uniform, standing far left.

# 2.3 Utopia and Revolution

## 2.3.1 The Danger of Utopia

Much — nearly everything — that has been accomplished by conscious and responsible human effort was, at first, a beautiful ideal, and nothing more.

349

The concretization of certain aspirations, like the demystification of certain formulas, is a task to which we must not fail to pay attention, which implies the need for greater social transparency, as well as more involvement and personal responsibility. This is necessary to avoid becoming a feeding ground for sparrows, who tend to care less about who sows the seeds than how they can devour them.

350

Recognizing that human nature is an artifice, and recognizing as well that we need to transform what surrounds us or what we may have achieved by birth or simple inheritance, it will be obvious that we must distinguish good ideas, as well as passing ideologies, from facts and the realities to which their acceptance or application

351

leads, otherwise we risk creating new alienations that could prove to be fatal, or at least unappealing, when enacted.

352 There are always those who dream of harvesting without sowing.

353 "Good ideas" in people who are unable to put them into practice can be a dangerous drug.

354 We need to overcome a false messianism, which amounts to a kind of blind hope that different formulas, which are more or less magical, and, of course, more comfortable, could change our fate. At any moment, the lottery, or simple luck, can change the prospects of an individual or a few people, but it is not possible for lotteries or luck to suddenly provide everyone with compensation greater than their own effort or sacrifice.

355 We talk a great deal about The People, but let us not forget that while it could be because of our desire to serve them, it could just as well be from our desire to "kidnap" them, to presume that one's own cause is identical to the desires or burdens of the people.

356 The people, too, have their passions and their mistakes; the people, too, flout justice and open the door to ambition or selfishness.

357 Utopias are inevitable, and, up to a point, useful. But we must not forget that "a utopia becomes reactionary if its creators try to impose their dreams on people against the public will."

358 The worst delusion that can afflict us all is to become in-

toxicated on simple words, and this danger is not simply hypothetical.

We must guard against utopian aspirations. Aspirations that deserve such a description, however rosy and flattering they may seem, are a disruptive element. 359

Admittedly, charismatic individuals or groups may come along, but what is important, when it comes to values like liberty and democracy, is that the charismatic people themselves respect what they claim to offer. 360

It is time for deeds, and not time for so many theories, whose practical realization bears little resemblance to the basic principles from which they start. 361

## 2.3.2 Revolution

Today, the revolution is called "participation." 362

Our people have always instinctively repudiated violence, even when they have found themselves swept up in it. 363

Salvation is not to be found on the path of violence and force. He who lives by the sword dies by the sword, as the saying goes. The path of violence will not raise the abyss, but dig it deeper still. At best, what will happen is that the sword will switch positions, so the handle becomes the blade and the blade becomes the handle. 364

365    Revolution is inevitable when processes have been blocked and evolution has halted. Reform is imperative as soon as the constant updating of the innovation process has been neglected even a little.

366    Revolution and violence resonate everywhere with growing intensity, but this is undoubtedly due to the fact that people are not satisfied with the processes of evolution and transformation.

367    People no longer believe in freedom, because they seek salvation in violence and force, which are irreconcilable with freedom.

368    Cursed be the grace that grants freedom, intangibility, and paper guarantees to the masses who have been robbed of their faith and denied those things without which it is impossible to eat, dress themselves, or care for their families.

369    A legend from the Middle Ages tells us of a sorcerer who had mastered the art of raising up fairies, who could do all manner of wonders and had all kinds of abilities. There was a curious youth who wanted to learn this art, and he went to the sorcerer and asked him to teach him the secret. The sorcerer did so, and the young man learned to conjure the fairies, but he was careless, and forgot to learn the secret of keeping them under his control. Once they were out of the hands of the sorcerer's apprentice, they acted with complete freedom and independence. And what happened? Simply, the fairies put an end to the sorcerer's apprentice, who was overcome by the skills and arts of his own progeny. Is this any different from what has happened to modern humanity? While it has learned to accomplish wonders and unleash the forces

of nature, it does not know how to master them, and becomes the first victim of its own works. When the development of a civilization does not begin with mastery and ongoing control over the forces of nature, the people are the first victims.

370 You could put an end to sin by putting an end to people, but do they deserve it?

371 Cooperatives, which must pay the greatest attention to people, must not idealize them, but see them as they are, with their defects and virtues. To cultivate cooperativism is to trust people, counting on their ability to attenuate their defects and fortify their virtues through their own attitudes.

372 Dangerous is the theory that makes one person a pedestal for another. To us, this is wrong.

373 The revolution or transformative management that starts by demanding that we surrender ourselves to it, bound hand and foot, is not and cannot be good. Promises that we will later recover the freedom, dignity, or participation we have mortgaged away can never dispel our doubts that this will happen.

374 Let us not forget the people, neither on behalf of the revolution, nor in the revolution, nor in the reconstruction.

375 It is a bad move, history warns us, to start by pawning our values, hoping to recover them later. Those most likely to win with this strategy are the least scrupulous, the adventurers and, always, the tyrants.

376 It has been said that tyranny needs slaves and the slave mentality is formed using all manner of resources that share a common denominator: replacing personal judgment with that of others, and training them to follow the orders of another without voicing an opinion or doubt.

377 The kidnappings of individuals that have received so much publicity lately must not lead us to forget those kidnappings that whole collectives and communities have suffered and suffer still.

378 It is obvious that without strength, it is not possible to obtain all that our conscience legitimizes and even requires. But to the extent that we have strength rooted in our conscience, in human unity and solidarity, we prioritize that strength and place it above the interplay and outburst of instincts.

379 Industrial cooperatives provide clear evidence that social progress and advancement, honestly sought, are the best path to building authentic social peace.

380 One is not born with dignity, rather it is created day by day, as we live in submission to profound and personal imperatives, achieving each one through sustained effort. This is the transfiguration that the revolution needs to avoid digging its own grave or reaching its end devoid of content.

381 We need a revolution based on work, not on myths. We must achieve unity based on truth and never on lies, hypocrisy, and error. We swim against the currents of "the consumer society that consumes," which would drug us with simple material well-being and reduce us to things on its balance sheets. The cooperative movement arises

among us, calls us together and helps us participate and act as people. And as people, we put our initiative, responsibility, and our creative capacity, to work, starting within the first cell or organism of creation and work, which is to say, the company. In this way, we can unleash a new drive to transform the economy and generate a new socioeconomic order, which is consistent with human dignity and the demands of human communities.

382 In short, Christ was a communist, if by "communist" we mean, "share your bread with the hungry, and shelter the poor and homeless," or if he commands that whoever has two coats give one to someone who has none.... But he did not command that anyone be stripped of their coat, nor that anyone could break into another's house and steal from them..., rather, he endorsed the natural principle of not violating the rights of others.

383 The economic revolution will be moral or it will not be. The moral revolution will be economic or it will not be.

384 A people is not born without history, nor is history made with hysteria. The community must pursue its health and physical and moral vigor, and will do so to the extent that it sees itself as obliged to act consciously and responsibly, knowing what is in its interest and what it costs. Using people is not the same as serving them.

Central offices of Caja Laboral/Euskadiko Kutxa (predecessor of today's Laboral Kutxa), 1961.

# 2.4
# Realism and a New Order

## 2.4.1 **Rationality**

We advocate rationalization and discipline that distance us from both resignation and uncontrolled rebellion.    385

Giving advice is not the same as giving wheat.    386

Everything can be improved upon, and reason must guide us when it comes to organizing work that has been entered into honorably and with incentive.    387

Reflection, pondering, rationality, and good sense are proof of a person's humanity.    388

Practicality, knowing how to act within a range of possibilities without diverging from or renouncing our ideals, has been one of our distinguishing features. We know how to unite in the common interest and not squander opportunities. Processes of association are only viable with moderation, with the consent of all, usually involving everyone having to sacrifice part of their    389 respective positions. Radicalization runs counter to the most constant qualities of our community and our people's human and social virtues.

390 We must face realities, rather than hypotheses, and reflect more on concrete data and facts than on purely ideological formulations.

391 We have realized that, yes, theory is necessary, but not sufficient: "We make the path by walking."

392 Good ideas are those that become realities.

393 Less triumphalism and more realism; fewer words and more deeds; fewer prophets and more people of their word; fewer dreamers and more practical people. Good ideas are the ones that can be turned into works, and good words are those that everyone knows how to back up with deeds.

394 We do not labor for gauzy idealism. We are realists, aware of what we can and cannot do.

395 With simple, easy projects, all we will end up with is balloons that deflate and fade away as soon as we reach them.

396 The fact that we do not live better is due not to a lack of knowledge, but of action. What we need most is to do more with all of our formulas for improving existence. We are no less endowed with faculties for doing than for thinking. We distract ourselves and even divide ourselves over things that are not really necessary either to think or to act, talking and arguing, comparing pure theories with realities. Is that not the case?

We start from the understanding that changes must be made to our way of thinking and our actions. We concentrate on the things we have hope of changing among ourselves, rather than the things we cannot change in others. — 397

Knowledge of problems is the first step to solving them. — 398

A basic, practical sense drives us to change what we really can change, and above all, to change that which, once transformed, could provide the best leverage for all kinds of further developments. — 399

We must accept servitude to economic laws with dignity, just as we do with physical laws, safeguarding the fundamental needs of our people in all cases. — 400

We have to comply with the present reality, even as we continue striving with all our strength to modify it, reserving and dedicating all our strength and resources to that end. — 401

To make progress, we must be able to confront problems and satisfy aspirations with common sense. — 402

Life — existence — is complex. Things are what they are, and not necessarily what we would like them to be. — 403

Whoever believes that there is only one problem in life is mistaken. Life is a fabric of problems. — 404

To be practical and consequential people, we have to put our hand to the reforms that can be made each day. — 405

406    The ideal thing is to do the good that can be done, not the good of which we dream.

407    We can all express an opinion, but those who are capable of work are the ones who will build the nation.

408    Great works are built stone by stone, with constancy and tenacity. Let us be capable of building. We build with our works more than our words.

409    Once more, let us remember that one way to solve big problems and serious issues is to address and solve one need at a time.

410    We affirm that ideas and guidelines can be good, or at least many of them, but facts and experience must not be scorned or undervalued, especially when they correspond to values that could justify those ideas. Experience is a form of legitimacy insofar as it corresponds to the imperatives of a mature, shared human conscience, to the extent that it leads us to accept a process of progressive liberation, and expanding justice, and, therefore, that we resolve to apply that experience on each successive rank and file of our desire.

## 2.4.2 Vision of the Future

411    So as not to cheat the present and not disappoint anyone tomorrow, we need to be efficient and practical. We will entrust ourselves to the judgement of time, and of the people who are resigned to play less glamorous or vocal

roles, which does not make them any less indispensable for the freedom and progress of our people.

If the task imposed on us by context or by life is arduous and difficult, all the more reason for those who speak of the good of the nation and its progress to keep in mind all their strengths and all their reserves. 412

Love for country must be shown by what we are all capable of doing, without expecting manna from heaven or solutions from "little Americans," even if they are native-born. [*Translator's note: "little Americans," or, in Spanish, "americanitos," refers to Basques who spent time working in the US, and returned with money and new ideas about how to organize industry, which Arizmendi did not share.*] 413

We will never wake up in heaven wondering how we got there. 414

Along with social laws, we must recognize the existence of other, economic, laws. 415

When the necessary economic resources are lacking, the best ideas and the best projects often remain at the idea stage. 416

Give a person a fish and they will eat for a day. Teach them how to fish and they will eat for the rest of their life. 417

Communities, like trees, grow to be vigorous and solid when they put down deep roots. The unseen roots of a community are well-made investments. 418

419   It is a historical constant: people are unable to actualize themselves and satisfy their aspirations without having to rely on time and their peers. Time and solidarity are basic factors, not simply accidental circumstances, for human advancement and social transformation. We have to sow or prepare to be able to harvest; to empower ourselves we have to be able to count on others and, consequently, give something, rather than always make demands.

420   Works and time—always and everywhere—are our trustworthy allies as cooperators, as long as we remain faithful to the principles of our communities of labor. Works and time, or, better said, and sufficiently: time, which only records our works.

421   Circumstances, in themselves, are neither good nor bad, simply a reality which we must take into account to be able to act upon them.

422   All times are bad for those who allow themselves to be overwhelmed by circumstances. We must know how to act in time to prevent this.

423   Let us remember that there are no coincidences, only consequences.

424   Heart and mind, discipline and judgment. Time will tell, and on we go. Justice and truth do not reside in time, but neither do they exist if they are not embodied.

425   Today, we are condemned to failure and sterility if we do not pay as much attention to what it takes to maintain continuous development around us as we do to our immediate needs.

It will not matter much that we are slow to be born, as people are, if we can be dynamic and strong in living and progressing.

426

The present, however splendid it may be, bears an expiration date, to the extent that it is disconnected from the future.

427

The future is not as uncertain as it is made out to be and more conditioned than it might appear, as much because we lose our interest in the future as because we try to shape it to our liking.

428

## 2.4.3 The New Cooperative Order

Being realistic and pragmatic does not mean renouncing ideals, which should not be confused with fantasies or lovely dreams, but accepted as goals to be achieved.

429

Insurrections are not good for communities. But nor should we put much faith in a peace structured in a way that does not provide possibilities of progress for all. It has been correctly asserted that today, the name for peace is "development."

430

We have agreed on the cooperative, considering it to be ideally suited for solving urgent problems of social development and progress and for making effective contributions to the campaign for another social and economic order, with all that implies. We have not presented the cooperative as a means of mere personal, much less indi-

431

vidual, advancement, or as a form of neglect of or disconnection from the community.

432 Cooperation is an authentic integration of people into the economic and social process, which shapes a new social order. Cooperators must collaborate in the pursuit of this end goal, joining forces with all those who hunger and thirst for justice in the world of work.

433 Cooperatives must not be closed worlds, but centers of social diffusion. We do not live in a world we have conquered, but on a battleground for social justice and a humane and just order.

434 The cooperative movement is sustained by a spirit of open solidarity. Its goal is far off and lofty: to build a cooperative regime, with solidarity on a global scale.

435 It is the destiny of humanity to dominate, modify, or transform nature through our reason, power, and virtue. We must build a new world and it must be, first and foremost, human. This world, custom-made for people, will be pleasing to God, who made us the rulers of creation.

436 The establishment of a new social order requires us to act in solidarity, not as an insurgency.

437 It is never too late for those who want to accomplish a concrete objective. It is enough to have dedication and total commitment.

438 Let us not think of other work structures, or of other organizational systems, with their risk of thinly veiled

abuses or tyrannies, if each member of the community is not prepared to deal with problems of this complexity.

Social servitude, which those of us who yearn for a new social order deplore, will not come to an end until each one of us feels greater concern for human learning and growth and the future of the children. 439

If we want to achieve a deep transformation of structures, if we want a new, more humane and equitable social order, we must demand first of all that the largest sector in our community have access to manufactured goods. To this end, it is better that they be freed from the need to provide themselves with other durable consumer goods exclusively at their own expense. 440

Nobody imagines that all truth or all justice could be settled in one simple battle, but some truth and some justice can. 441

We need solidarity between regions. So, those who manage the common good and everyday citizens, too, are obliged not to defend their privileges as developed provinces but, instead, to behave with great openness and great solidarity. 442

A healthy society is one in which everyone lives according to his or her own merits, and where it becomes more and more difficult to live at the expense of others. 443

Cooperative entities have to be elements of progress, development, and the promotion of a new social order. 444

Arizmendiarrieta at work in 1941, newly assigned to parish service in Mondragón.

# 2.5
# The Cooperative Enterprise

## 2.5.1 The Cooperative Spirit

Work is the solid base for development and advancement. Unity is the lever that multiplies strengths of each one. Cooperation is, for us, a system of solidarity that makes work into the best means of personal and collective advancement. — 445

The enterprise is the primary economic-social cell, and in it, we have established the fundamental relationship between labor and capital in such a way that the person, which is to say, human capital, is not only the most important engine of the economy, but also its goal. — 446

Enterprises are made by people — people with both technical and moral capacity. — 447

The cooperative enterprise is a living organism; it is a society of people in a community supported by solidarity, and awareness of this solidarity is the driving force in which we must trust. — 448

449  A cooperative is a structure in which labor and people are the sources of power, and capital has an instrumental and subordinate character.

450  The cooperative movement is an economic endeavor that takes the form of educational action, or an educational endeavor that uses economic action as a vehicle for transformation.

451  It is not possible to establish a suitable organizational policy that is conducive to the advancement of such a broad base of collaborators without a thorough review of the current status, both mental and administrative, of the owners as well as the workers.

452  Cooperativism is not about changing a company's owners or managers, but transforming its nature and social function.

453  Cooperation summons people to collective work, but each person bears their own responsibility. It is the development of the individual, not against others, but with others. The objective is the person — not its monstrous development as a being determined, or at least susceptible to the determination, to crush others — but rather, the development of what is the best and most sacred within the individual. It is something close to us. Cooperativist philosophy rejects both the collectivist and the liberal conceptions of human nature. It recognizes the unique value of the individual, but insists that the individual cannot be totally him or herself without entering into creative, spiritual, and materially productive relationships with the world to which he or she belongs.

Cooperation has no place for rootless people; it is not a nest for migrating birds.  455

Anyone who joins a cooperative should not go in thinking of their own advancement as something to be desired and attained with no need to think of others.  456

Just as capitalism's least appealing feature has come to be the trafficking and gambling of capitalists without capital, so we must recognize that, in the eyes of others, the most intolerable aspect of cooperativism may be the presence of cooperativists without solidarity or objective communitarianism.  457

Cooperation is the unity of people who have learned to accept limitations on their individual wills to the extent required by the common good.  458

The acceptance and development of the cooperative idea must obey another motive, another perspective. The strength of this movement and its moral standing are rooted in something else: cooperation and the association of people must be seen as a realization and expression of the law of solidarity and as the basis for ever-accelerating progress. Our ideal as cooperators must be the realization of authentic human solidarity, as God wishes, enabling people to progress in all aspects of life.  459

To embrace cooperativism is to believe in solidarity, and those who believe in solidarity can no longer put limits on the scope of its application. Human solidarity is an active and powerful ferment, a force that multiplies as the circle of its application widens.  460

461 Our cooperatives must primarily serve those who wish them to be bulwarks of social justice, and not those who see cooperatives as refuges or safe spaces for their conservative inclinations.

462 Our integrity, our solidarity, and our will to improve can open up perspectives that may seem like a dream today, but for those who know the economic and social realities of the present are nothing of the sort.

463 Cooperativism is the affirmation of faith in people, in work, in integrity, in human harmony, turned towards constant and progressive advancement.

464 We cooperators have in our minds the idea that the future society will probably have to be pluralist in all aspects, including economics: the state and the private sector, the market and the planned economy, various entities, be they paternalistic, capitalist, or social, will be combined and coordinated. If we really believe in and love people, their freedom, justice and democracy, we will need to treat each situation, the nature of each activity, the level of evolution and development of each community, on the basis of an approach that is overarching but not exclusive.

465 What is good about cooperativism is that it tries to make people face their problems, not on their own but in solidarity, united with others.

## 2.5.2 Cooperative Management

The fact that we prioritize human values over purely economic and material factors does not mean that the enterprise can or should lose any of the potential benefits of efficiency. Rather, this should lead to greater efficiency and quality. 466

We must begin by recognizing the need to make business management more socially aware, to orient it and enable it to operate with new structures and goals. 467

A society that seriously intends to plan the development of human greatness needs a sufficient staff of competent people who are willing to take on positions with the greatest responsibilities and highest standards without insisting on a standard of living for themselves and their family that is higher than that of the rest of the people. 468

In the complex field of industrial production, cooperative entities that intend to survive crises need expert and agile leaders, members who must have the most deeply ingrained sense of service and generosity, and be capable of steadily resisting the countless temptations that will appear along the way. 469

These make a good match: leadership committed to developing the people under their authority, and a community that gives them broad trust. 470

In a chain, each and every link is indispensable, and it matters relatively little where in the chain they are. Something like this happens in a community that is well-conceived and properly developed. 471

472   If the fortunate and privileged minorities or the radical and systematic non-conformists take exception, that should not be an obstacle, but a spur to a more rigorous loyalty to the social principles that inspire the cooperative, and a fully shared regime of participation and management validated by its efficiency.

473   The common good normally depends more on the degree of discipline and mutual trust among the cooperative members than on the successes and errors of its leaders, who, in time, may be relieved of their posts. It is wiser to have a certain tolerance for the latter than to look on the former impassively.

474   Competent subordinates eventually end up forcing the removal of incompetent authorities.

475   Blind trust is a poisoned gift.

476   The art of good leadership consists of making sure each person occupies the position or performs the activity for which they are best suited.

477   Let us give the general assemblies the attention they deserve and the life they need.

478   Cooperation is incompatible with any degree of human servitude. People, as such, cannot be exposed to forms of subordination that compromise their human values.

479   We cooperators must stand out for our capacity for commitment, for the degree of foresight, planning, order, and forward thinking that we are capable of applying in our management.

Insufficient organization should not be confused with respect for freedom. 480

We are obliged to be a community of workers, but also of merchants. It is necessary to have markets to buy goods and sell others. In other words, exchange is vital in our situation, and with exchange comes dependency. We must make this dependency viable through the exchange of our products, and the more appealing they are to others due to their quality and other selling points, the more viable the interdependence between equals or friends will be. 481

The management and highly qualified staff who guide the cooperative have the greatest responsibility for ensuring that cooperation fulfils the objective of introducing a sense of solidarity into the framework of the enterprise, not in response to any pressure, but out of appreciation for cooperative doctrine and the sense of justice that the working world demands today. 482

Good navigation of a ship on the open sea requires expertise, involves foresight, and may demand audacity and risk-tolerance, and therefore, a calm authority. 483

That is to say, to ensure the validity and currency of democratic and humanist principles in the economic and social order, the cooperative enterprise must identify itself as a public enterprise, community-driven and managed, with an open structure and with mechanisms enabling the integration of intellectuals and professionals appropriate to the historically necessary technology. 484

We need our cooperatives to be authentic enterprises, with rates of productivity and efficiency competitive 485 with those that other entities achieve with different economic structures.

486 Cooperativism without the structural ability to attract and assimilate capital equal to the demands of industrial productivity is a temporary solution, an outdated formula.

487 We have renounced the capitalist system, but not the need for capital in ever-greater amounts.

488 It is risky to make each cooperative a closed world. We have to think of inter-cooperative solidarity as the only recourse to address other problems of growth and maturity. We must think in terms of a living space appropriate to our circumstances.

489 The cooperative movement needs to sink its roots — roots of solidarity, justice, and freedom — deep in the spirits of the people who are committed to our grassroot organizational units, such as our work communities. But, at the same time, the movement needs to proceed with the transformation of other entities in the economic, financial, social, and political spheres, consistent with the original spirit of the movement.

490 The waters that resign themselves to being held back or simply accept being in a reservoir do not forsake their natural destination, which is the ocean. They still arrive, undiminished, with the advantage that — having been subjected to the reservoir's system of life and engineering — they fertilize new fields and turn large turbines, producing energy and fertilizing the land as they go, without any loss to the flow of water that the ocean receives. We, the people, can continue to obtain everything

we obtain today from their resources, while at the same time achieving a new effectiveness, a new fertility, simply by organizing their use or administration a bit. The Caja Laboral Popular is the dam, the administration system that will enable us to use our resources, modest as they may be, with the advantages that organization and administration can undoubtedly offer, first and foremost in terms of maximum solvency and order, but also in terms of fluidity or, to use the technical term, adequate liquidity for our deposits or savings.

## 2.5.3 Workers and Entrepreneurs

People are human to the degree they are social. It could be said that the desire that is common among cooperative members — to be entrepreneurs more than proprietors — owes itself in part to this condition. 487

A cooperator is not just a worker but also a business owner. 488

All are owners and all are entrepreneurs, without discrimination, in the good times and the bad, providing the capital they have and the work that is needed. 489

The workers, who up to now have defended their interests by making collective demands, must continue to strengthen their position with a conscious and planned involvement in economic life, occupying themselves not only with consumer goods, but productive goods as well. 490

495     It is not enough for us for society, understood as some anonymous, amorphous collective, to be the owner of the chickens, if it is possible for us to be so, personally or in solidarity, on a human and communal scale.

496     We should not treat the company like someone else's laying hen, only aspiring to enjoy the eggs.

497     The coming of age of the working class will have been affirmed when, as a class, it takes a firm position on the possession of the means of production and consequently exercises its influence in all domains of the economy.

498     To take seriously the duty of work and everything that can be derived from it is the best testimony of adhesion and respect to the great legion of workers of our time and in our case. We who have proceeded to organize work by ourselves according to our conscience, its dignity, and its rights, have a greater responsibility to leave a positive record showing what workers are capable of doing, demonstrating that they are sufficiently mature to take part in the management of socioeconomic activities, with all their political implications.

499     It is imperative that we be resolved to be more than relatively fortunate consumers. We must also become investors, because as mere consumers, all we are doing is giving to our exploiters with one hand what we try to take from them with the other.

500     We have two hands, and we must accept responsibility for two functions that need to be in step: the consumption necessary to replenish our strength and compensate for our efforts, and the investment that is indispensable if we are to look to our future and build a solidarity that

continues from generation to generation. For us to be able to play this role as investors, we need unity as much or more than we may have needed it to ensure a decent livelihood.

If we do not place our trust in emancipatory projects that lack an economic base, and if we intend cooperativism to be a true liberation of the worker, we must accept the economic involvement and responsibility required that our entities require to stand on their own feet. 501

We must have faith in our power, in the power of our unity, our solidarity, our involvement in all social and economic life, and not relegate ourselves to second-class status. 502

The decisions that workers make each time they proceed to make a deposit, to open an account or place their savings in the social institutions that represent them, can serve to promote a new social order as much as or more than many other social and political measures. We could even claim that, today, workers can make a greater impact as savers and investors than as citizens or trade unionists. Of course, to reach the height of their power, both as savers and investors and as citizens and trade unionists, they need an organization. 503

Workers today need to weigh their economic power, and the possibilities for action they have through well-managed investment. 504

It is we cooperators who can put an end to the notion of the immaturity of workers. We need to dispel the doubts people have of social democracy, which is often presented as an impediment to the economic progress necessary to 505 adequately satisfy the growth and progression of human needs.

506 We affirm the capacity of workers to organize themselves in accordance with principles that offer maximum responsibility and maximum consideration for the dignity of people.

507 Workers are not second-class citizens. We must end the practice of infantilizing workers, as if they always needed others to make decisions for them in particular competencies and times and places. Therefore, there is no reason to continue considering their resources or savings as something that requires special supervision. Their funds are property, identical to that of other citizens, and as property, they entail risk and responsibility.

508 It is not enough to avoid personal servitude while running the risk of falling into collective servitude.

509 Our biggest fear for the cooperative future is the danger that cooperators might allocate more to consumption than is prudent in any given situation. The capitalist world that surrounds us can rest easy the day that it sees us living a life of privilege, because the decline in our investment rate or the weakness of our enterprises will mean the decline of our expansive and combative strength, and at the same time, the rupture of our solidarity with the working world.

510 We constantly face the old temptation of Esau, who sold his birthright for the dish of lentil stew. Workers' rights and hopes for a new order cannot escape this temptation, that of making choices and gaining short-term advantages.

511 — The biblical choice between an inheritance and a dish of lentils is constantly being placed before us, presenting itself at different historical moments of evolution with different external nuances or features.

512 — Comfort, ostentation, luxury, and waste are the outcome when development is regarded as a goal, rather than a means and a starting point for progress and human and social well-being.

513 — What kind of drug is money? To obtain it, each of us studies, works, and becomes clever. Many respectable things are invoked, like the dignity of the person, the right to humane labor, and the demands of social justice. These are forgotten as soon as we have money and begin to use it, or to prostitute it, or exchange it for some trinket or whim, thinking it is enough to say, "It's mine, and I can do what I want with it."

514 — Let us not forget: cooperatives and cooperators will continue to succeed as long as they do not fall behind in the human training of their members and in the progress of capitalization, always ensuring that their respective activities can be carried out at an adequate level.

515 — We must bear in mind that to create industries in underdeveloped communities, we cannot start with abstract ideas of just wages, etc. People who have no capital must learn to spend less than they produce.

516 — Austerity, in the form of savings, is a must if we wish to achieve development that is meaningful and harmonious.

517 Clearly, saving money is a noble virtue, which always appears surrounded by other virtues, by many virtues.

518 The credit union is essential to the cooperative movement. This is the way for working people to do their part to support the cooperative movement.

519 Rates of investment, with the empowerment they entail, will one day provide the best evidence of our solidarity with others, and we know that those rates of investment only exist to the extent we are able to withhold some resources from immediate consumption.

520 The modern enterprise needs not only start-up capital but permanent financing, based on renewed efforts and sacrifices.

521 The greater the self-financing, the greater the dynamism of the company, and the more ambitious the goals it can achieve. We sacrifice the present to the future, the person to the collective.

522 It follows from nature, from education, and from practical use: self-financing is at the center of the multiple rights that must be recognized, secured, and organized with the participation of all stakeholders.

523 Education, work, and savings seem so different that treating them as one issue might seem to make no sense. However, we have to consider them as three dimensions or aspects of one problem, the problem of the social advancement of people and communities.

524 The great leap forward of a developing society can come to nothing, if savings and investment are lacking.

Savings and work are yesterday and today joined together, or with unbroken continuity; past generations lending a hand to the present one; the sacrifice and effort of yesterday that pay off today, or the sacrifice made today that we will bless tomorrow.

We are workers and owners, as we often say. No less owners than workers, precisely because we have chosen to free ourselves from the limitations of the world around us.

We worker-owners can and should have a place of honor in the development of our nation, and in the management and resolution of its problems. Above all, we must be able to leave a record showing that today the workers have the necessary maturity, their emancipation is happening, and cannot be held back due to any supposed immaturity or lack for preparation. Work is a shield and a fortress that is always ready.

## 2.5.4 An Experience in Perpetual Development

The communities of our region have a great capacity for work, a strong sense of association, significant common and practical sense, for which the Basque people are well known, and a rich abundance of small and large community institutions with the most diverse social objectives, so they can perfectly understand this call for advancement.

However, so far, all this wealth and potential value in our communities has not been given a natural and appropriate channel, because no one has known how to interpret it or, if you like, no one has known how to give it specific expression, a manifestation that translates into specific institutions or entities around which to galvanize a project and justify commitment.

529    We draw heavily on so many possibilities that were forgotten, squandered, or rejected, by people who wanted to and could not, who dreamed and woke up unable to start down the path they dreamed of. So many vocations without opportunity.

530    Cooperatives are not born to foment social insurrections nor to deteriorate into bourgeois strongholds, but to keep human and social values alive and operational, in the heart of an ancient people with a tradition of resistance and a capacity for renewal, who deserve better luck.

531    Cooperativism must be considered a vanguard element of the workers' movement, and all workers must be able to benefit from the results of cooperative training and administrative experience, which will help them better understand and address their problems.

532    Cooperativism is not an end, but a means. It is an institution, the ideal instrument for embodying in economic and social life ideals whose goodness no one who is honest and noble-minded can dispute, or at least, they have the acceptance of most.

533    Cooperatives solve some problems, not all problems. Let us measure their value by the problems they solve, and by their potential to address ever broader and deeper ones.

We have the feeling that for some people or groups in our region, cooperatives are a kind of target, something to be dismissed or disparaged, for motives that are not as respectable and worthy as these critics pretend. The workers in our region are teaching an important lesson, demonstrating their capacity to build, the direct contributions they make to the development of the country, and the viability of alternative methods of organization of labor and social relations. · 534

Our cooperativism is being built by the formal cooperators and the anti-cooperators as well, all of us who are, in the end, members of a community, parts of a single people. · 535

The enemies within are those who, like microbes, destroy life and bring death to the living organism. · 536

What may be most important in these early days of cooperativism is not what you do, but what you try to do. · 537

The radicalism of the cooperative approach to development, which calls on us to battle on multiple fronts, labor and economics, the personal and the communal, means that either we succeed or we fail utterly. It presupposes strong spirits or, at least, people who are willing to risk it all. For this reason, it is not the right formula for everyone, but the biggest mistake we could make is to set our demands at a level accessible to the weakest among us, which would make it impossible to reach higher levels. · 538

In general, those who are not able to carry out successful projects in another organizational or legal form are not the people who should set up cooperatives and launch themselves into life as agents and subjects of change. · 539

540 Without some risk, nothing can be achieved.

541 Cooperativism is fundamentally an organic process of experiences, characterized by service to moral values, by the prevalence of people, as such, over the other, more instrumental, factors of all economic processes and activities.

542 Cooperativism is an organic process of experience in which human activity, socio-economic activity, is inspired and governed by higher human values.

543 Efficiency for efficiency's sake is not synonymous with humanism.

544 Cooperativism is a living doctrine and position no matter how you look at it. With respect to its possibilities, we should not shrink from the simple fact that in the past, its achievements have been short-lived. The hegemony of any doctrine or system is based on education, and our entire educational system and, consequently, our entire institutional framework, have been highly antagonistic to communitarian affirmations. While indulging and encouraging individualistic positions, they have profound reservations about proposals for freedom and human solidarity.

545 The cooperative movement will be a passing phenomenon unless it spreads and develops in the broader social context, and consequently takes root in the field of education and social and economic relations.

546 This experience corresponds to a new spirit of trust in people and their capacity. In this case, it revives the sense of freedom, dignity, and justice, which are clearly

manifested in the traditional and democratic institutions of our land and, therefore, are examples of the specific character of its people.

One of our characteristics has been our practicality, our ability to seize possibilities without being passive or renouncing our ideals. We know how to join together and not squander opportunities that are in the common interest. Our processes of association are only viable with moderation, as consented to by all, with members usually having to sacrifice something of their personal positions. Radicalization is contrary to the most constant qualities of our community and to the human and social virtues of its people.

As exponents of the spirit of a people more prone to action than to speculation, a loving people, jealous of their freedom and their privileges, and solicitous of the vital space in which to realize themselves in work and through work, to contribute to the benefit of all, this is what we affirm and desire: being more than having, progressing more than dominating.

547  The cooperative must be reconstituted and renewed every day.

548  This is where our cooperative attempts originate: a group of associations created by workers in freedom and honesty.

# Afterword:
# Cooperation and Liberation

*Jessica Gordon Nembhard*

Don Jose Maria Arizmendiarrieta is inspiring for many reasons. He was a leading thinker in what we now call Liberation Theology, but more, he connected community-based education and training with the need for social economic development, economic democracy, and the dignity of work to achieve human liberation. Arizmendi's new cooperative order integrates the social and the economic. The purpose of an economy is to enable people to live full lives. He was his own kind of political economist, understanding that an economy is only as strong as the people in it, and solidarity strengthens people.

My first association with Father Arizmendiarrieta's philosophy and work is about the importance of education for cooperativism. The first Mondragon worker cooperative was started by students who graduated from the first class of the community-run polytechnical high school that Father Arizmendiarrieta founded. He stressed the importance of community-controlled education, learning to self-manage and to develop responsibility, and learning how to work well with others. In my own research about cooperatives I have found that good cooperators and strong co-ops start by people learning and training together. This develops shared understandings as well as solidarity among co-op members or potential members. I found this to be a similar pattern for how most of the Black co-ops in the US started—with community-based or school-based or religious-based study groups. In the study groups, they learned how to start and run cooperative businesses, they connected with other Black co-op societies and organized study tours. They then established working committees and buying clubs, and then started co-op businesses. For the most successful co-ops, education and joint learning continue indefinitely. The Mondragon Cooperative Corporation went on to create an entire cooperative K–12 and university education system. Arizmendi built that foundation.

Both the Basques of northern Spain and African Americans experience contradictory relationships in their societies as national minorities—citizens without full citizenship rights, experiencing long histories of exploitation, inequality, and social ostracism. Father Arizmendiarrieta taught that subaltern people do not have to live subaltern lives. They can take charge of their own lives, be warriors for change. We can work together and fashion a new society that delivers prosperity for all through worker cooperatives. Not many people understand economics as a project of human liberation. Father Arizmendiarrieta showed many that it is—or can be.

Father Arizimendiarrieta recognized the importance of gender equality and collaboration. He argued that the value of work is independent of gender. At one point he noted that the position of women in a society is an exact measure of a society's level of development. This liberation project must liberate everyone.

We also learn from Father Arizmendiarrieta that cooperativism is an experience—it's a process of practice and praxis, a way of life. Economics and work are often very alienating. We have to leave our humanity at the door to the factory. But Arizmendi did not accept that. He argued that we are all economic agents. We must be captains of our economic journey and stewards of our community's economy. And we must do this as human beings, working with purpose and dignity, in solidarity with others for the greater good. Social cooperation, concern for community, and economic solidarity — shared values and shared work — enable communities to address specific economic issues in ways that build on their existing assets, create new economic structures, and develop democratically-controlled enterprises. This is a lesson for all of us, to recognize the power of solidarity and unity; and embrace transformation.

From reading Father Arizmendiarrieta's writings we feel his love and respect for human beings, human dignity, and human equality. He commands us to pursue those through cooperativism in order to develop economic solidarity regimes that benefit everyone equally, transform hierarchy into democracy, restore the dignity of work, and collectively liberate humanity.

# Bibliographical Note

All the sentences and reflections collected in this compendium have been taken from the collection of writings of Don José M. Arizmendiarrieta, by J. M. Mendizábal/Caja Laboral Popular, which comprises fifteen volumes (one printed, 1978, and fourteen photocopied in a restricted edition, undated). In this collection, the writings of Arizmendiarrieta are arranged according to a thematic classification with seven main sections, which we indicate below with the corresponding abbreviations:

| | |
|---|---|
| CAS (only printed vol.) | Social Apostolate Conferences |
| CLP (I, II, III) | Caja Laboral Popular |
| EP (I, II) | Professional School |
| FC (I, II, III, IV) | Cooperative Education |
| PR (I, II) | First Accomplishments |
| SS (I, II) | Homilies |
| V | various |

The quotations in this anthology are numbered so that the interested reader can always consider the excerpted quotation in its full original context. The numbers refer to the aforementioned collection of writings by Arizmendiarrieta. Thus, the first reflection cited here corresponds to the number 1, which in the index below refers to PR I, 11. This citation system should be understood as follows:

1 PR I, 11. First Accomplishments, vol. I, p. 11.
2 EP II, 3. Professional School, vol. II, p. 3.

Here is the original source for each of the quotations:

# 1 People and Society

1. PR I, 11
2. EP II, 3

## 1.1 THE PERSON

3. SS I, 166
4. EP I, 60
5. SS II, 35
6. CLP III, 62
7. FC II, 171
8. CLP III, 250
9. EP II, 8
10. FC II, 26
11. EP II, 292
12. EP I, 47
13. SS II, 268
14. PR I, 106
15. SS I, 185
16. EP II, 328
17. EP I, 20
18. EP I, 298
19. FC II, 27
20. FC II, 76
21. FC II, 26
22. SS II, 243
23. EP II, 338
24. FC IV, 152
25. FC I, 116
26. FC II, 190
27. FC I, 124
28. FC III, 294
29. EP I, 327
30. FC I, 98
31. FC II, 206
32. CLP III, 28
33. FC I, 103
34. FC II, 110
35. CLP III, 269
36. SS II, 258
37. SS I, 60
38. EP I, 51
39. SS I, 146
40. FC III, 83
41. FC III, 168
42. FC II, 9
43. EP I, 167
44. FC IV, 180/181
45. PR II, 15
46. SS I, 182
47. SS I, 161
48. EP I, 29
49. SS I, 160
50. SS I, 173
51. SS I, 173/174
52. FC II, 46
53. EP I, 228
54. FC II, 244
55. PR I, 116
56. PR II, 148
57. FC I, 141
58. PR II, 155
59. PR II, 155
60. PR I, 186
61. PR II, 150
62. PR II, 154
63. PR II, 159
64. PR II, 159
65. PR II, 79
66. PR II, 138
67. PR II, 106
68. PR II, 83
69. PR II, 105
70. PR II, 83
71. PR II, 85
72. PR II, 139
73. PR II, 41

## 1.2 FREEDOM

| | | |
|---|---|---|
| 74 CLP I, 232 | 84 SS I, 112/113 | 94 CAS, 213 |
| 75 CLP I, 234 | 85 CLP I, 274 | 95 SS I, 276 |
| 76 SS I, 60 | 86 FC IV, 29 | 96 CLP III, 165 |
| 77 FC II, 244 | 87 FC IV, 207 | 97 FC II, 163 |
| 78 FC II, 125 | 88 SS II, 147 | 98 FC I, 200 |
| 79 FC IV, 173 | 89 FC I, 253 | 99 FC II, 31 |
| 80 FC II, 8 | 90 FC IV, 30 | 100 FC IV, 19 |
| 81 FC IV, 176 | 91 FC IV, 85 | 101 CLP III, 111 |
| 82 FC I, 327 | 92 SS I, 255 | 102 FC I, 200 |
| 83 SS I, 113 | 93 FC III, 178 | |

## 1.3 RESPONSIBILITY

| | | |
|---|---|---|
| 103 FC IV, 173 | 112 CLP I, 199 | 121 SS II, 30 |
| 104 FC IV, 175 | 113 FC IV, 225 | 122 SS I, 127 |
| 105 FC IV, 197 | 114 CLP III, 178 | 123 PR I, 106 |
| 106 FC IV, 195 | 115 FC IV, 12 | 124 FC I, 328 |
| 107 FC III, 235 | 116 FC IV, 40 | 125 FC I, 251 |
| 108 PR I, 98 | 117 CLP II, 63 | 126 FC IV, 138 |
| 109 CLP II, 100 | 118 FC I, 232 | 127 FC IV, 149 |
| 110 FC II, 237 | 119 CLP II, 45 | |
| 111 CLP II, 99 | 120 CLP III, 263 | |

## 1.4 MORALS

| | | |
|---|---|---|
| 128 FC IV, 88 | 136 FC I, 200 | 144 FC IV, 141 |
| 129 FC I, 233 | 137 PR II, 16 | 145 FC IV, 98 |
| 130 FC I, 233 | 138 FC I, 52 | 146 FC III, 161 |
| 131 EP II, 72 | 139 PR II, 19 | 147 CLP III, 248 |
| 132 SS II, 258 | 140 FC I, 233 | 148 FC I, 325 |
| 133 EP I, 27 | 141 SS II, 5 | 149 FC IV, 44 |
| 134 FC I, 200 | 142 CLP I, 284 | 150 SS II, 307 |
| 135 SS I, 181 | 143 CLP III, 28 | 151 SS II, 70 |

| | | |
|---|---|---|
| 152 SS II, 266 | 158 SS II, 141 | 164 SS II, 243 |
| 153 SS I, 218 | 159 SS II, 143 | 165 FC IV, 120 |
| 154 FC IV, 138 | 160 SS I, 103 | 166 SS II, 134 |
| 155 FC I, 201 | 161 FC I, 233 | 167 SS I, 166 |
| 156 SS II, 223 | 162 SS II, 127 | 168 PR I, 178 |
| 157 SS II, 71 | 163 SS II, 241 | 169 SS I, 214 |

## 1.5 EDUCATION

| | | |
|---|---|---|
| 170 SS II, 95 | 190 FC I, 322 | 210 SS II, 93 |
| 171 CAS, 159 | 191 FC I, 156 | 211 EP II, 202 |
| 172 CLP III, 248 | 192 FC I, 321 | 212 CLP I, 50 |
| 173 CLP III, 187 | 193 EP II, 335 | 213 EP I, 64 |
| 174 EP II, 258 | 194 EP II, 336 | 214 EP I, 64 |
| 175 EP II, 107 | 195 FC II, 110 | 215 SS II, 94 |
| 176 SS II, 89 | 196 EP I, 84 | 216 EP I, 269 |
| 177 CLP III, 269 | 197 EP I, 247 | 217 EP II, 258 |
| 178 EP I, 22 | 198 EP II, 4 | 218 CLP III, 121 |
| 179 EP II, 71 | 199 EP I, 256 | 219 EP II, 262 |
| 180 FC II, 77 | 200 SS II, 99 | 220 EP II, 91 |
| 181 EP I, 19 | 201 CAS, 103 | 221 FC I, 91 |
| 182 EP II, 260 | 202 CLP I, 50 | 222 EP II, 109 |
| 183 EP I, 19 | 203 EP I, 272 | 223 EP II, 86 |
| 184 CLP III, 248 | 204 EP I, 228 | 224 FC II, 23 |
| 185 CLP III, 248 | 205 CAS, 103 | 225 FC II, 133 |
| 186 EP I, 271 | 206 EP I, 117 | 226 FC II, 111 |
| 187 EP II, 336 | 207 EP I, 335 | 227 FC I, 89 |
| 188 EP II, 188 | 208 FC I, 323 | |
| 189 EP II, 4 | 209 SS II, 95 | |

## 1.6 THE SIGN OF VITALITY

| | | |
|---|---|---|
| 228 CLP III, 249 | 231 EP II, 64 | 234 EP I, 229 |
| 229 EP II, 52 | 232 EP I, 146 | 235 EP II, 330 |
| 230 EP II, 88 | 233 FC IV, 126 | 236 PR I, 121 |

| | | |
|---|---|---|
| 237 CAS, 25 | 246 FC I, 238 | 255 CLP I, 208 |
| 238 SS II, 252 | 247 FC III, 181/182 | 256 CLP I, 238 |
| 239 CLP III, 59 | 248 FC III, 161 | 257 CLP I, 145 |
| 240 CLP III, 38 | 249 FC III, 158 | 258 FC I, 218 |
| 241 CLP III, 265 | 250 FC III, 63 | 259 CLP II, 99 |
| 242 FC I, 320 | 251 PR I, 97 | 260 FC IV, 216/217 |
| 243 FC II, 10 | 252 PR II, 15 | 261 CAS, 25 |
| 244 FC III, 304 | 253 EP II, 10 | 262 CLP I, 257 |
| 245 FC III, 216 | 254 CLP I, 281 | |

## 2 Work and the Cooperative Enterprise

### 2.1 WORK

| | | |
|---|---|---|
| 263 PR II, 99 | 273 FC I, 95 | 283 CLP I, 275 |
| 264 EP I, 298 | 274 FC I, 130 | 284 CLP III, 267 |
| 265 FC II, 138 | 275 FC I, 142 | 285 CLP III, 266 |
| 266 FC I, 25 | 276 CLP I, 190 | 286 FC I, 246 |
| 267 CLP III, 3/4 | 277 EP II, 107 | 287 PR II, 143 |
| 268 FC III, 307 | 278 FC I, 76 | 288 PR II, 81 |
| 269 FC II, 169 | 279 EP I, 116 | 289 PR II, 146 |
| 270 FC IV, 112 | 280 CAS, 94 | 290 EP I, 41 |
| 271 FC II, 138 | 281 FC I, 161 | 291 EP I, 232 |
| 272 CLP III, 68 | 282 EP I, 206 | |

### 2.2 UNITY

| | | |
|---|---|---|
| 292 CLP III, 123 | 299 FC I, 86 | 306 CLP I, 234 |
| 293 FC I, 155 | 300 SS II, 260 | 307 FC IV, 152 |
| 294 EP I, 198 | 301 FC II, 34 | 308 EP II, 73 |
| 295 PR I, 98 | 302 FC I, 322 | 309 CLP I, 249 |
| 296 FC I, 15 | 303 CLP I, 108 | 310 FC I, 310 |
| 297 PR I, 171 | 304 CLP III, 21 | 311 FC I, 307/308 |
| 298 FC I, 103 | 305 CLP I, 232 | 312 CLP III, 126 |

| | | |
|---|---|---|
| 313 EP I, 84 | 325 FC III, 196/197 | 337 CLP III, 149 |
| 314 SS I, 224 | 326 FC II, 243 | 338 FC III, 233 |
| 315 CLP I, 99 | 327 FC III, 244 | 339 CLP III, 110 |
| 316 CLP III, 13 | 328 FC I, 66 | 340 FC IV, 179 |
| 317 FC I, 268 | 329 FC II, 7/8 | 341 CLP III, 114 |
| 318 FC II, 72 | 330 FC II, 165 | 342 FC IV, 179 |
| 319 EP I, 68 | 331 FC II, 195/196 | 343 FC I, 312 |
| 320 EP I, 201 | 332 FC III, 8 | 344 FC II, 56 |
| 321 CLP III, 269 | 333 FC I, 232 | 345 FC I, 311 |
| 322 CLP I, 87 | 334 FC I, 182 | 346 FC I, 311 |
| 323 EP II, 120 | 335 FC II, 237 | 347 FC I, 312 |
| 324 PR I, 107 | 336 FC I, 241 | 348 CLP I, 133 |

## 2.3 UTOPIA AND REVOLUTION

| | | |
|---|---|---|
| 349 CLP I, 269 | 361 CLP III, 264 | 373 FC IV, 73 |
| 350 FC III, 312 | 362 CLP I, 200 | 374 CLP I, 296 |
| 351 FC III, 312 | 363 FC IV, 113 | 375 EP II, 118 |
| 352 FC III, 327 | 364 SS II, 152 | 376 EP II, 118 |
| 353 FC II, 156 | 365 FC II, 10 | 377 FC IV, 112 |
| 354 CLP I, 50 | 366 FC IV, 70 | 378 CLP I, 284 |
| 355 FC IV, 222 | 367 SS II, 147 | 379 CLP III, 65 |
| 356 SS I, 214 | 368 SS II, 150 | 380 CLP I, 221 |
| 357 FC IV, 142 | 369 SS II, 259 | 381 CLP I, 223 |
| 358 FC IV, 51 | 370 FC IV, 69 | 382 SS I, 10 |
| 359 CLP I, 38 | 371 FC III, 177 | 383 FC II, 246 |
| 360 EP IV-2, 118 | 372 CLP III, 264 | 384 EP II, 119 |

## 2.4 REALISM AND A NEW ORDER

| | | |
|---|---|---|
| 385 CAS, 225 | 390 FC IV, 156 | 395 CLP II, 100 |
| 386 FC IV, 222 | 391 CLP III, 263 | 396 FC IV, 229 |
| 387 CLP III, 225 | 392 EP II, 181 | 397 FC IV, 65 |
| 388 FC IV, 176 | 393 FC III, 327 | 398 FC III, 207 |
| 389 CLP I, 235 | 394 FC IV, 65 | 399 FC IV, 112 |

| | | |
|---|---|---|
| 400 CLP I, 37 | 419 FC IV, 42 | 438 EP II, 335 |
| 401 CLP I, 126 | 420 FC IV, 76 | 439 PR I, 187 |
| 402 FC IV, 87 | 421 CLP I, 86 | 440 FC II, 117 |
| 403 EP II, 116 | 422 EP I, 119 | 441 FC IV, 222 |
| 404 PR I, 201 | 423 EP II, 151 | 442 FC I, 333 |
| 405 PR I, 106 | 424 FC IV, 224 | 443 FC II, 69 |
| 406 PR I, 74 | 425 FC II, 21 | 444 CLP I, 141 |
| 407 FC III, 256 | 426 EP II, 182 | 445 FC II, 7 |
| 408 CLP II, 100 | 427 CLP I, 273 | 446 FC II, 166 |
| 409 PR I, 213 | 428 EP II, 116 | 447 FC I, 63 |
| 410 FC III, 312 | 429 FC IV, 207 | 448 C IV, 182 |
| 411 FC IV, 137 | 430 CLP I, 196 | 449 FC II, 166 |
| 412 CLP III, 221 | 431 FC III, 302 | 450 FC III, 95 |
| 413 CLP III, 221 | 432 FC I, 302 | 451 CLP III, 63 |
| 414 EP I, 204 | 433 FC I, 253 | 452 FC I, 262 |
| 415 FC I, 53 | 434 FC I, 306 | 453 CLP I, 143 |
| 416 CLP III, 24 | 435 FC I, 36 | 454 CLP III, 38 |
| 417 EP II, 22 | 436 CLP I, 90 | |
| 418 CLP III, 61 | 437 EP II, 37 | |

## 2.5 THE COOPERATIVE ENTERPRISE

| | | |
|---|---|---|
| 455 FC I, 166 | 468 FC II, 25 | 481 CLP I, 275 |
| 456 FC I, 64 | 469 CLP III, 154 | 482 FC I, 248 |
| 457 FC III, 316 | 470 FC I, 122 | 483 FC I, 215 |
| 458 FC I, 52 | 471 FC II, 97 | 484 FC III, 151 |
| 459 CLP III, 9 | 472 FC IV, 115 | 485 FC II, 193 |
| 460 CLP I, 155 | 473 FC I, 276 | 486 CLP I, 38 |
| 461 FC I, 63 | 474 FC I, 69 | 487 FC I, 164 |
| 462 CLP III, 3 | 475 FC III, 287 | 488 FC I, 196 |
| 463 CLP I, 147 | 476 FC I, 118 | 489 CLP I, 128 |
| 464 CLP III, 65 | 477 FC I, 169 | 490 CLP III, 10 |
| 465 FC II, 64 | 478 FC I, 131 | 491 CLP I, 179 |
| 466 CLP III, 250 | 479 FC III, 232 | 492 FC II, 217 |
| 467 FC III, 185 | 480 FC III, 168 | 493 CLP III, 158 |

| | | |
|---|---|---|
| 494 CLP III, 147 | 513 FC III, 311 | 532 EP II, 4 |
| 495 CLP III, 141 | 514 FC II, 23 | 533 FC III, 302 |
| 496 CLP III, 139 | 515 EP II, 219 | 534 FC III, 300 |
| 497 FC II, 40 | 516 FC I, 236 | 535 FC III, 65 |
| 498 FC III, 292 | 517 FC I, 28 | 536 SS II, 191 |
| 499 CLP II, 135 | 518 FC I, 305 | 537 FC III, 65 |
| 500 CLP III, 135 | 519 FC II, 192 | 538 FC II, 191 |
| 501 FC I, 329 | 520 FC III, 35 | 539 CLP III, 153 |
| 502 CLP III, 134 | 521 FC III, 254 | 540 CLP III, 12 |
| 503 FC I, 304 | 522 FC II, 170 | 541 FC II, 190 |
| 504 FC I, 303/304 | 523 CL PI, 49 | 542 FC I, 14 |
| 505 FC I, 302/303 | 524 FC IV, 11 | 543 FC IV, 63 |
| 506 CLP III, 3 | 525 CLP I, 53 | 544 CLP I, 147 |
| 507 CLP III, 129 | 526 FC III, 292 | 545 FC II, 23/24 |
| 508 FC I, 330 | 527 FC III, 259 | 546 CLP I, 241/242 |
| 509 FC II, 22 | 528 CLP I, 118 | 547 FC II, 192 |
| 510 FC II, 40 | 529 CLP III, 269 | 548 CLP I, 247 |
| 511 FC III, 124 | 530 CLP I, 279 | |
| 512 FC III, 310 | 531 CLP I, 109/110 | |

www.ingramcontent.com/pod-product-compliance
Lightning Source LLC
Chambersburg PA
CBHW071256070526
44583CB00017B/2503